SACRED DANCE

WISDOM FROM LEADERS LIVING A SOUL-LED LIFE

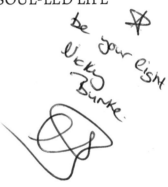

be your light

Vicky Bunke.

SANCTUARY PUBLISHING

CONTENTS

To all the teachers, mentors & guides who have divinely guided the way for each one of us to walk our unique path.

INTRODUCTION

Living a soul-led life is every individual's birthright. It is an opportunity for you to connect back to the intrinsically curious piece of yourself that remembers you are walking with the support of Divinity.

At some point in our journeys, we get engulfed with our human experience, and we forget that there is a piece of ourselves that is our soul. Your soul is the piece of yourself that is a fragment of the whole, whether you call it God, Source, Spirit, Universe, etc.

When you feel re-connected to your soul, you remember you are here for a greater purpose.

That you are a piece of Divinity embodied.

That you are far greater than you'll ever be able to see with your own two eyes.

Tapping into your soul's presence is tapping into your limitless potential.

Your ability to co-create a life that is led by the hands of grace.

But along the way of this remembrance of your innate self, you are still being called to walk this path of your human self.

To feel. To enjoy. To experience.

To hurt. To die. To be reborn.

All of it is a part of the journey- your soul incarnated here for a reason.

It was not only for you to remember who you are, which is a soul being.

But also to have a full spectrum human experience.

The dance between the two brings fulfillment to your existence here.

The yin & the yang of remembering & forgetting.

The Sacred Dance of your journey.

I am so excited to share with you the fierce healers, thought leaders & visionaries that have said yes to living a soul-led life. May their stories be an opportunity to feel into the true potential that lies within you.

For many to take the leap to walk alongside the sacred in this life- will take courage & faith in yourself as a soul-being that is a part of the entire web of Divinity. A sense of internal safety to be cultivated is the beginning of the journey for most, to start to remember who they truly are rather than who they have been told to be while deepening trust with Divinity. May these stories be a mirror of safety within.

By reading this book, may you start to follow the breadcrumbs calling you to trust the way forward that is different from what you expected. These internal nudges is your soul beckoning you to come back home.

May these stories show you the sheer magnitude that can happen when you do indeed trust yourself.

To walk your unique path forward.

To remember your limitless potential.

To experience the fullness of your human experience.

May these stories mirror to you what is truly possible when you say yes to living a life that feels like a Sacred Dance.

Annette Maria
Founder of Sanctuary Publishing

ANDREA BLINDT

FROM FEAR TO FEARLESS

*T*he cold hard metal of the loaded pistol pressed into the side of her head, causing her to wince. He'd returned home from work drunk. "You better pray this baby is a boy. It's the only thing stopping me from pulling the trigger," he said, as he threw the plate of food, which she had spent hours cooking, all over her and the kitchen floor. His rotten teeth showed as he smiled, while his words slid cryptically into her ears. As the baby grew inside her, it continued to absorb the energy of terror, fear, grief, and despair as they pulsed through the lifeline that connected the two.

* * *

HER BODY SHOOK UNCONTROLLABLY as she was rolled into the delivery room for an early c-section. This baby was unplanned, being conceived a few short months after her first child was born, which caused her concerned doctors to insist she deliver early to prevent rupture of her uterus. She felt powerless, certain that the baby was a girl despite the grainy black and white sonogram that showed otherwise. The baby was stuck, afraid to move forward into this world, causing the doctor to physically force it out of the womb. It was placed on a cold hard table where bright fluorescent lights shined on its naked body, revealing the identity to everyone. That baby ended up being a girl, and that girl is me.

* * *

THE ENERGY in my childhood home was toxic, heavy, and full of physical pain. When I was almost two years old, my mother finally escaped her abuser. She fled with my older sister and me in the middle of the night, carrying a trunk of belongings and the hope of a safer future with her. Time passed with us frantically looking over our shoulders in search of the bad man who wanted to get us. The terror of being hunted transformed my mother, causing her to become an angry, scary monster herself. With no safe space for me to exist and feeling like a burden, I eventually taught myself how to vanish. I felt unworthy, unwanted, and unloveable every day of my life. I blamed myself for being a girl, believing that if I had just been a boy, I would have been happily welcomed into my family, and we wouldn't be living life on the run.

I began working to prove my worth to my mother and society, longing to be accepted. I never knew that this desire was being driven by the fact I had been unwanted since the day I was conceived. I started to hide all of myself in order to survive, and in doing so, I inadvertently told myself that I truly was unworthy and unlovable. How could anyone possibly love me if I wasn't even capable of loving myself? I buried the girl I was created to be in this world and became a robot moving through life in order to survive my existence. I did all the things that were expected of me both at home and in society, molding myself like clay in order to fit into the exact box I was asked to squeeze into. I meticulously worked, moved furniture twice my size, cooked dinner, and cleaned without ever being asked. I excelled academically, graduating high school with honors and attending college locally, where I finished at the top of my graduating class in nursing. I was chosen out of a thousand applicants for a pediatric oncology position at a prestigious hospital, where I continued to work towards earning my place in society. I got married, bought a house, and worked to start a family. I persevered, flying through the never-ending checklist waiting to be seen, valued, and loved, not understanding that those accomplishments would never bring me peace, happiness, or the connections in my life I desperately longed for.

I was afraid of what pushing against the grain in my family and society would look like, so I persisted, creating a life that the world said was "right". I complied with every request my husband and society made of me and ignored the agonizing pain I felt in my body. That pain was a signal, an alarm begging for me to stop, to slow down, and to acknowledge the brilliant women within me eager to be found and embraced. Sadly, I was too focused on if the world thought I was worthy and lovable to acknowledge the little girl that had been buried deep within my soul.

I was miserable. My subconscious programming ran the show, and all of my actions affirmed them. As a child, I survived immense physical, emotional, and mental abuse. And as an adult, I was experiencing similar traumas, but my environment looked different. I couldn't understand what was happening. My conscious brain went through my checklist, looking for where I had failed, where I had accidentally deviated from the path. I believed I must have done something wrong to cause all of this suffering to exist. I carried that false narrative into my world, accepting that I truly was unworthy and unlovable. I had done all the "right" things; life was supposed to be good, to be easy, to be less painful, or so I thought. Except it wasn't.

My hardships continued, and the pain in my body became unbearable, forcing me to stop and acknowledge it. I was plagued with autoimmune disorders, chronic pain, and debilitating depression. The memories that had been buried in my body from a lifetime of misery were becoming too great to contain any longer, and that once strong container weakened, threatening to break. It took two miscarriages, multiple surgeries, a turbulent IVF cycle, the traumatic deaths of my twins, and the dissolution of my marriage for me to finally implode.

That night had been like so many others before it. My husband

3

was working overtime, and I was putting my 15-month-old daughter to bed. We finished reading, singing, and applying coconut oil to my abdomen before sealing it with a kiss and patting the little baby inside goodnight. I was pregnant again, and my body felt on edge. The fear of losing another baby after the tragic loss of my twins terrorized me. It took everything inside me to stay present and not escape into fear. I gently kissed my daughter's cheeks and walked into the living room, exhaling as I collected the mail and sat on the couch to sort through it all. As I separated letters, I paused, realizing I had accidentally opened a letter addressed to my husband. I had been on autopilot, my mind wandering while my hands tore through the envelopes in order to organize the contents. I set the envelope aside and continued moving through the pile until a constant ache in my stomach pushed me to focus on the white envelope again. My husband's name was handwritten, and I found it odd that there was no return address.

We had experienced a lot in our short marriage together. The loss of our twins and the fear associated with each subsequent pregnancy tore further into our already fragile relationship, causing tensions to rise and the divide between us to grow. Curiosity continued to build inside me until, eventually, I took the envelope into my hands and pulled the contents out to analyze.

As I slowly read the letter, heat coursed through my veins, igniting my body in what felt like a blaze of fire. The letter revealed devastating consequences for the actions my husband took; behaviors that negatively impacted the health and well-being of our family. At that moment, I was forced to make difficult decisions for myself and my small children. I was afraid of the ripple effect my choices would create. I knew society would frown upon me, that I would be seen as a failure again, which further fueled my "not enough" fallacy.

I took the letter into my hands and inhaled, walking slowly into my daughter's bedroom. I hovered over her angelic sleeping body and absorbed her as the beautiful gift she was in this world. It had been a huge effort to be able to bring her successfully into this world, and I was determined to make her life happy and full of joy. I moved from her bedroom into my bathroom, slowly closing the door behind me.

Once inside, I collapsed onto the cold bathroom floor. Tears carved a path towards my chin, where they trembled before propelling into a puddle on the floor. My breaths were sharp and jagged, forceful, and reckless. I hugged my knees, lying in the fetal position as I watched the scenes my subconscious mind had locked away to project a story available only now for me to see.

I saw myself as a child, skinny and bruised, with dull vacant eyes staring back, longing to be seen, to be touched kindly, loved, and accepted as the gift I was. I saw my husband and acknowledged the excitement I felt at being able to check another task off my list of things to do that would bring me closer to my perceived fulfillment. I explored all the red flags in our relationship and recognized the fear of being alone that caused me to dismiss them. I watched myself on our wedding day as tears filled my eyes and an agonizing ache squeezed at my stomach, trying to alert me of the dangers ahead. I noticed myself silence that alarm as I took a deep breath and walked down the aisle towards my future husband. I witnessed the failed fertility cycles I had survived, two miscarriages, and then a successful twin pregnancy after a complicated IVF cycle. In amazement, I saw my body soften and noticed hope fill my being. I watched as I started to welcome hope into my life and exhale into it. I allowed myself to dream and envision a future I would love to live. And then, I watched as a brutal reality presented itself to me again. I noticed similar emotions surrounding me that mirrored the ones I felt the day I was born. I shook uncontrollably as I was rolled into an emergency c-section, uncertain of the outcome. I was afraid, silenced, and felt unworthy of being heard. I was forced to deliver my twins early, against my will, by a doctor who was not my own and knew nothing about my babies or me. I saw the woman I once was sitting weakly beside two incubators, absorbing the perfect, small bodies inside that were weighed down with tubes and wires made for sustaining life. Tears continued to flush out of my body as I watched myself bravely hold my beautiful babies for the first time, allowing their perfect soft skin to meld into mine. I experienced the heaviness enter my life again as they took their final breaths and left this world. I watched as I masked my pain in order to plan their celebration of life ceremony, and then pick up the miniature boxes of ashes that contained their precious remains. I experienced the agony of another IVF cycle that resulted in my current high-risk pregnancy, not fully knowing how our future would now look. I allowed my tears to cleanse my soul, and after exploring the trials of my past, I paused. In that silence, I pondered my life, my values, and the dreams I envisioned for my family. They were different now, slightly tinged but full of new potential. Honoring my deep knowing, feeling incredibly empowered, and not worrying about what the world would say about me, I asked for a divorce.

Shortly after separating from my husband, I ended up in the hospital for 6 long, painful weeks. I was on bedrest and full of uncertainty. Fighting for the sweet baby that was growing inside me, while missing my beautiful toddler who was at home wanting her momma. It was a challenging time for us both, but in that hospital room, isolated from the world and my soon-to-be ex-husband, I was able to sit even more in my emotions. I found ways to explore them and allowed space for them to teach me what they were there to help me with. Mentally, I was exercising an area that hadn't been utilized in that capacity before, while physically, my uterus was stretching and growing to accommodate my baby as he grew larger. I felt physical pain and was flooded with fear, not knowing if my body could carry him to a safe gestation. I worked to push through mental barriers, focusing on the outcome I desired, which was my baby, alive, healthy, and thriving. That vision carried me through weeks of agonizing physical and emotional pain. The idea of burying another baby was worse than any physical pain I could ever endure. So I pushed forward, masking my pain and inching closer to the delivery date. Eventually, the constant pain became a loud scream as my uterus slowly ripped open. My doctors prepped me for an emergency c-section. As I was moving onto the operating table, I felt my pain decrease, and peace filled my body. I smiled excitedly, telling my medical team that I no longer needed to deliver; the pain was gone. Upon hearing this, my doctor's words became rushed. He shouted orders into the operating room, and the medical team jumped into action. As the doctor cut into my abdomen, I could smell burning flesh fill the air, and then his voice once again, "Oh my God, oh my God, I can see his face, his face is here… I haven't cut the uterus open yet.. the cord is wrapped around his neck… three times.. your uterus ripped… we could have lost you both…you could have bled to death..you both could have died." The horror of the delivery shook me to the core, but the euphoria I felt when I saw my precious baby and heard his small cry was a balm that soothed my soul.

Grateful to be alive, my son and I returned home eager to create new memories. Once settled, my husband moved out, and it became the three of us: my daughter, my son, and me. Free from the weight of my marriage, I started to heal and grew stronger than I ever had in my life. I was excited and started to believe I was capable of achieving anything. I plastered affirmations on every wall of my house and learned to speak with love and authority. My kids and I were thriving, and joy radiated from our home. As I continued to heal my body and mind, my vibration lifted and the embers inside of me were reignited. Those embers became bright flames, shining like the light on a light-house, guiding my now-husband safely towards me.

When I first met him, I was fearful about what society would say about the timing of this new relationship. My body clung to the memory of my past hurts, perceived failings, and the potential risks of starting another relationship. I had to relearn a lot, teaching myself how to feel safe, receive love, and live life in a way I had never imag-ined or seen modeled to me. In the end, I decided to take the path I had never traveled; a direction that led me toward compassion, curiosity, and hope to create a life full of possibilities for my children and me.

Easing into the safe space my new husband offered, I fully explored my discomforts instead of running away from them. I learned how to listen to the small whispers that lived deep inside my body instead of the loud chatter of the world around me. I filled my body with foods and thoughts that healed my ailments and allowed me to naturally create and birth two new lives, despite the limits doctors placed on me and without the assistance of fertility treatments. I learned how to embrace my husband's unconditional love without looking for the strings that were attached to it, and I allowed myself to experience a blessed life.

Through this, I was able to find the path that led me to where I had hidden myself as a little girl. I found compassion for that precious child who had spent a lifetime hiding and performing in order to survive her environment. I offered her grace instead of ridicule, acceptance instead of judgment, and understanding instead of disapproval. I honored the trials she had faced and praised her for the grace she showed as she bravely overcame each devastation. In this sacred space, I saw the beauty I truly possessed. Despite my upbringing and the traumas that threatened to bury me, I had survived. In that place of deep acceptance, I learned how to surrender, asking myself for forgiveness and promising to never abandon myself again. Full of love for the beautiful woman I am, I proudly rose, shining my light into the world for myself, my family, and those suffering to see.

My desire for you is that you would feel worthy, wildly capable of achieving all your dreams, and strong in your ability to create a life you love living. You are not alone, you are a masterpiece, and you are deserving. I encourage you to forgive the past, feel gratitude in the present, and create positive expectations for the future, but above all, I encourage you to live life in the moment. To throw the checklist away and to make time for you. You are loved, you are worthy, and you are more than enough. You don't need to suffer silently. Growth can be painful, but I assure you, arms will be outstretched, ready and willing to receive you if you fall.

ABOUT THE AUTHOR

ANDREA BLINDT

Andrea Blindt is a Registered Nurse, Holistic Health Practitioner, Published Author, and Inspirational Speaker.

She uses her healing journey to bring wisdom and hope to her patients. She understands that each person is unique, much like the root cause of the obstacles they encounter.

After her son received an incurable diagnosis, Andrea studied various healing modalities that changed the outcome of his life, and are a valuable resource to the patients she serves through her successful nursing practice: Growing Miracles with Andrea.

Andrea inspires others to reclaim their power, advocate for what is in their best interest, and learn the tools needed to be able to make decisions for themselves that are in alignment with their beliefs.

She has been featured on Natural Health Radio, Conceive IVF, and is a contributing writer for a parenting magazine. She lives in sunny California with her dreamy husband and four beautiful children.

Website: www.andreablindt.com
Instagram:www.instagram.com/andreablindt
Email: heal@andreablindt.com

ANNETTE MARIA

THE GOLDEN THREAD

"It is important to expect nothing, to take every experience, including the negative ones, as merely steps on the path, and to proceed."- Ram Dass

*L*iving life as a sacred dance is a journey of remembering. Remembering who you innately are- that you are a part of the Divine whole and always guided along the way. This story is one of me following the golden thread that continues to guide me on a soulful journey.

When I was in 8th grade, I started going to the gym when I was a chubby child- exercise was a solution to "fix" me. Of course, being very young, I was unsure what to do once I got there, so I started to find myself in the yoga room. I was so pulled to the practice and how I felt upon completion. In that room is where I remember picking up my golden thread. This golden thread is the internal guidance from my intuition that would continue to lead me forward in my life. The seed was planted that yes, there was another way to be, connect and explore life within myself.

As I saw the worn path proclaimed to be the "right"- I knew deep down I was always meant to live life in some different way. I knew my life wouldn't look the same as those who walked before me. But I didn't have any idea what it would look like. Naturally, I started to try to figure it out while blending my way into the herd, moving forward.

Fast forward to fall of 2017, I was one year into my first corporate job designing wallpaper. I just graduated from my yoga certification and was determined to make it a fruitful side hustle. After a few months of juggling, I was done trying to balance both. I was truly miserable in my day job and totally in love with teaching classes.

I proclaimed to God, setting the intention of wanting to teach yoga full-time. Two weeks later, I was fired alongside two other co-workers. Walking out of that building, a box with my belongings in hand, I knew that I was given another piece of my golden thread to follow. Repeating thank you God, thank you God. I knew I was about to embark on a journey; little did I know my golden thread would be taking me down into the depths of the Lower World. I was about to meet deep layers of shadow and trauma that made me question my ability & made me believe that I needed to be someone other than myself to thrive in this life.

When embarking on a soul-led journey, you cannot avoid or transcend your human experience. Your human experience is vital to living out your soul's mission. Consumed with depression and anxiety, I didn't know where to turn. I was stuck. I was sitting in a daily swamp of muddy waters, unsure how to stand back up. I found myself deep in the darkness, asking myself why I would be given the answer to my prayer, the freedom but I couldn't figure out how to teach yoga full time. I was in a state of forcing my way to make my dreams happen, as I was used to previously, with nothing but stagnation finding its way to me. I found myself upset and confused about my ability to co-create with God that I found myself trying to co-create something negative and harming to myself- to prove that I can actually make something happen. Twisted, I know, but it was all that I was able to make sense of at that moment.

Whenever I would drive my car, I would think about getting hit by a deer. I was asking God to hit me with a deer to show me I was being listened to. Christmas Day 2017, driving from my partner, George's family gathering to my brother's, we were hit by a deer. Thankfully we were both safe and okay. The deer ran away as well. It was yet again a piece of my golden thread-

A wake-up call that I was asking for.

Yes, I am being listened to, but I need to stop forcing my way forward.

* * *

LITTLE DID I know I needed to be stopped fully to really look at who I was before going deeper on my path of service. I was stopped by losing my job and then getting hit by a deer- exactly what I was asking for, but my expectations made it hard for me to see I was in a potent phase of my growth. I was deep in spiritual practice and self-inquiry but I was truly staying at the surface, simply stopping at the awareness. My opportunity to deepen was here- to look at the pain, suffering, and running I was living in. I grew up in a home where I experienced trauma & abuse in many forms. Thinking I had a "normal" childhood - whatever that means - I accepted I did not.

I got to face the sadness of the little girl within me that felt abandoned and felt like she was not wanted on this Earth. I got to face all the anger bubbling up under the surface of never being able to have a playful childhood. I got to face the disgust, feeling physically and emotionally violated along the way. Knowing I was being asked to face these memories and feelings, I felt stuck yet again. At that time, I thought asking for support was weak, looking up therapists, giving them a call and then hanging up.

Thinking I am a failure, look at me fired from my 1st "real job", living in my parent's basement, with nothing to do & I can't even make it through the day without an anxiety attack. The spiral went deeper. I couldn't go into the public, drive my car or even go to a job interview without being in total panic. I would teach yoga classes while having full-blown panic attacks, fearing of fainting at any moment.

Fainting was a coping mechanism I picked up early in my childhood to help me escape from the depths of pain I felt. Often, when we are faced with deep traumas, we develop coping mechanisms to allow us to continue living on this Earth. For me, it felt like living here was too much, so when I felt overwhelmed or panicked, I would start to go down the rabbit hole of fearing getting dizzy, which would lead me to either get dizzy and faint or lay in bed with a racing heart not sure what was wrong with me. At the time, I didn't realize it was a response to my layers of suffering, I thought I would have to live with this for the rest of my life.

I would keep trying to talk my way out of the monsoon of thoughts drawing me down, but I felt locked. I thought, well, if you wouldn't ask for help, you will need to get yourself through this and that was exactly what I did. Tending to my trembling heart and anxious mind, I found myself spending time sitting in my childhood bedroom talking to the girl who was so sad living there. I found myself surrendering more and more to this is where I am, but I know I won't stay here forever. I started to explore shaking practices and yin yoga to bring my nervous system into a relaxed state. But I still felt hopeless, thinking I was all alone- I was wondering when I would get out of this and start feeling better. Wanting to just move on and run away rather than be in the moment.

One day, I was reminded that I was far from alone- the energy of Lakshmi, the Goddess of Abundance, came to me to chant her mantras. Ah, the golden thread presented itself again. An exhale. So I followed it, I started to chant, Om Shri Mahalakshmi Namah, and express myself in a new way. I started to feel the love of God in my heart again. I started to feel the love for myself again. Slowly following the golden thread out of my first dark knight of my soul. I'm so proud of that version of myself that walked me out, but I also feel sad that she thought she needed to do it alone. She inspired me to further support others, so they never had to feel how I felt. Nowhere to turn because I didn't want to get forced onto medication and go down the route of traditional talk therapy at that time.

As I started to chant more daily, I felt my heart opening back up. A deep connection to my Feminine essence was reignited- the desire to sing, play & create. I would find myself starting to dance more and wanting to create. I would get guidance to write and later publish a children's book, The Worry Wave and create jewerly. These pieces of my soul got stuck in the traumas, pain, and abuse that occurred and stayed there until it started to feel safe to come back.

Slowly I started to create a sense of safety for myself.

The self I knew myself to be, rather than the self I was conditioned to be.

Growing more and more trust in my golden thread, my divine guidance led me to continue on my unique path. It led me to become a massage therapist, quickly realizing the depths of what the body holds on to, I started to go deeper into studying the body. I remembered how much shaking my body was the only practice to mellow my anxiety. And all those moments of getting emotional during yoga class or during a massage. I knew there was a greater depth I was able to walk my clients into. I knew that massage was only a part of the path but was not forever. When I felt the Divine call to leave it behind as the pandemic began, I knew my sacred path was unfolding deeper.

In 2020, I officially started my own business facilitating coaching and energy healing virtually on a global scale. In that time, I started to dive deeper into studying somatic healing, utilizing the medicine of my body to help me process deeper layers of trauma. But this time, I didn't do it alone; I had a team of support from a therapist, energy healer & business coach. I started to remove myself from the "Miss. Independent" identity that I knew was just another coping mechanism that helped me for so many years but was no longer needed.

Entering into 2021, feeling supported and ready- I felt another call from my golden thread to leave my healing business as I knew it behind me. I knew I would be guided towards something better. The trust I have developed within myself is that I am being guided to either what I am asking for or something better. But it doesn't always make it easy for my ego to follow suit to what I am being called to follow.

I was scheduled to go on a trip to Costa Rica to deepen my knowledge of somatic healing when I heard a clear call to cancel the trip. Another hard pill to swallow, but I listened. The week I was supposed to be in Costa Rica was the week I signed up to be a part of a dear sister's multi-author book journey called Legacy Speaks. Being a part of that multi-author book sparked something within me to start Sanctuary Publishing, the juicy golden thread that led me to a massive expansion in Self. That led me to be sitting here writing a chapter in this book my publishing company has curated.

As I dived deep into Sanctuary Publishing and holding space for soul-led leaders in feeling safe for being seen in sharing their story to the world, I knew it was a break I needed from holding space for others in an intimate healing container but little did I know, that I would be facilitating deep healing work within my publishing house. The potency that was set forth within, the healing and transformation that individuals would go through writing their stories as well as sharing them to the world. The magnetism that they felt being safe doing it was a piece of the puzzle I wasn't able to see when I said yes to picking up this golden thread. Merging somatic and energy healing with publishing is the medicine I share here.

And that is the beauty of saying yes to a golden thread is that you cannot see the full picture of what you are setting forth, but you know deep within you it is your divine next step. It may not always make sense and be crystal clear, but clarity comes alongside listening and action. I feel and have been told many times that if you knew the full scope of where you were headed, you wouldn't say yes to the journey. I believe that is why we are given those beautifully curated golden threads if we choose to see them as so - they are a moment that God is asking you- Do you trust walking in the darkness with my light leading you?

That does not mean that the light will not pull you into the depths of your human pain and darkness, and it does not mean that life will always be easy. It is asking us to see the grace within it all. No matter your current reality, it is a curation for your highest evolution and growth, even if you can't see how at this moment. There is an energy of detachment calling, asking you not to get swept up in the momentary high or low but to focus on the grand overall design of your soul's mission here.

When I was deep in my dark knight of the soul in 2017, I would have told you it was the worst year of my life, but looking back at it, I can say it was one of the best years that shaped me into who I am today. Not undermining the pain I felt but having a bird's eye view of what was occurring now. I was able to find my own strength. I was able to develop an unshakeable energy of trust in God. I was able to truly start walking my soul's unique path forward on this Earth. Without that time, I would not have been able to find that within myself.

I invite you to check in with yourself if you are familiar with your golden thread or want to deepen your relationship in following it-Where are you being guided to next?

The voice or feeling that feels subtle, oceanic and peaceful. It may not make logical sense, but it makes a whole lot of heart-centered sense. I invite you to start listening and acting upon it. Start small, start to develop your own understanding and trust and never stop listening. Even in moments when you think it is crazy to listen, continue. Continue choosing and loving yourself through it all. I believe listening to your own internal wisdom is how you start to carve your unique path, the one your soul was meant to be living in this life.

What is next for me?

This thread is pulling me to dive deeper into developing my personal connection to God and opening my spiritual gifts in a whole new way. I am being called to be more of service in person and starting to deepen my evolved intuitive healing practice alongside Sanctuary Publishing. I've never felt more excited to be on this Earth feeling safe within myself & knowing I can trust my soul's guidance. As well as the hands of grace which continue to feed me my golden thread that is leading me to being of deeper service on this Earth.

Living a soul-led life doesn't mean you know your grand plan for life, as society tried to teach you is what you need. Which usually leaves us feeling underwhelmed, like, okay, great, I know what the next 60 years of my life will look like, and then when I retire I will start living. Society's "right" path is one rooted in a false sense of safety. It makes you put your trust outside of yourself, draining you of your power. I say f*ck it, pick up your golden thread and start trusting your self above all else. You know what is right for you. Your soul will guide you if you choose to listen and start walking the path that keeps you dancing in the polarities of existence. Fear and love. Excitement and anxiety. Control and surrender.

Dear soul, please know you are never alone in carving your own path forward. Lean into the support and love that is all around you and within you. When you enter into the moments of darkness, there is a time to face it yourself, and there is a time to ask for a hand to support you. Know that you will be guided to exactly those meant to walk alongside you on your path.

Reclaiming living a soul-led life is one of putting the faith back in yourself. It is walking into the dark abyss of the unknown, scared at times but also excited because you know the golden thread will always guide you into one hell of a ride. Cheers to your journey of remembering who you are, a limitless soul embodied in a finite being here to allow magic to happen.

ABOUT THE AUTHOR

ANNETTE MARIA

Annette Maria is the Founder of Sanctuary Publishing, Somatic Soul Guide, Best Selling Author & Host of Sacred Dance Podcast. Through Sanctuary Publishing she merges healing with publishing. She works with soul-led entrepreneurs who are ready to be authentically seen for their medicine whether it is through publishing their story or refining their mission. Alongside her publishing house, she runs an intuitive healing practice where she is a Somatic Soul Guide. Guiding individuals ready to be leaders in their lives into the wisdom of their body through Somatic Healing, Sound Healing, Energy Work, and Intuitive Guidance. She is an advocate for everybody learning how to listen to their inner truth & feeling invigorated to live it out! Annette's vision is to see the planet as a place that supports each individual in feeling wildly expressed while living out their soul's purpose. She resides in New Jersey with her artist partner, George & rescue dog, Max.

Website:
www.activationsbyannette.com
Facebook:
https://www.facebook.com/annettemaria123

Instagram:

https://www.instagram.com/its.annettemaria/

Insight Timer:

http://insig.ht/annette.activator

Sacred Dance Podcast:

https://anchor.fm/annette-maria

Email:

hello@activationsbyannette.com

ASHLEY HOLMES

LIGHT WITHIN

The light within me dimmed when my brother, Steven, died. I felt like a part of me was lost forever. That life would only get better if he was still here. That moment changed me and the trajectory of my life forever. In an instant, I grew up. I was no longer a child, even though I longed to be. My faith in life was nearly extinguished.

I lost trust that the world was a safe place to be. I allowed myself to become invisible and dissolve into the abyss of grief and sorrow. I wanted my reality to be anything other than what I woke up to on a daily basis. There was always that bittersweet moment upon waking before remembering that he was no longer present.

I spent years trying not to feel any of it, to numb it, to escape it, to push it beneath the surface and pretend it wasn't there. I went so far as living part way around the globe in New Zealand, hoping that a change of scenery would mean that all was not lost. I was trying to see if there was a shred of hope that there was more to life than pain and suffering. Life had fallen apart after he died. Initially, we all pulled together in our grief, but everyone's way of coping was completely different, and we all became versions of ourselves I no longer recognized. My family of five had become a lone venture, and I left as soon as I could after graduating from high school.

I was drawn to New Zealand, and I continued to go back there. The vibe and the culture were so laid back, and it was like stepping back in time. The oceans were so inviting, cleansing and healing. The people were unlike any I had met before, so friendly and down to earth. My love for children grew and grew as a nanny because I could relate to their innocence, sweetness, and curiosity. They were so good at living in the moment and loving unconditionally. I feel like I have had a unique and special relationship with every child along my path. I see them for who they are and love them for what makes them special.

I met and later married my husband in New Zealand. Stu proposed after 6 months and broke down the walls I had created around my heart to protect myself and keep me safe from experiencing any pain. We were meant for each other from the moment we met. He makes me a better person and has always valued what is truly important in life. His love is like no other, and I am beyond grateful to have found my soulmate.

I remember being out one day in NZ and my stomach sinking. I returned home to a message saying my step-brother was in a coma. Paul did not survive his injuries, and I jumped on a plane home to be with my family and say goodbye at his funeral. I had enough awareness and was in a healthier place in my life and knew that I just needed to feel it and spend three weeks just being with my family and processing another loss.

I was full of fear boarding the plane back to NZ. Worried that everything would fall apart AGAIN like it did the last time. That everything that was stable in my life would disintegrate into shambles as it had before. We proved our relationship was legit and moved to Canada after we were married. Feeling as if I was here that it would make a difference, that everyone's happiness was dependent on me. I was still naïve to the fact that I was not responsible for anyone else's emotional state, nor was I the glue holding us all together. I wore a burden that wasn't my responsibility, but internally it felt like it was.

We began trying to conceive after we had settled into being on Canadian soil. I kept thinking that it would just happen like it was 'supposed' to. I was young and healthy and in my 20's still, so it would happen naturally. Time kept ticking, and no missed cycles – I was regular like clockwork with no glimmer of hope. I decided to see a counsellor as I thought perhaps the issue was beyond the surface. I never once mentioned infertility to him because I was in denial that it was my current operating reality. If I spoke it out loud, then it would be real, and I would have to talk about the fears I had of never being able to have a baby. I also didn't broach the subject because I didn't feel like it would land well with him. He told me there was no point continuing our sessions, and I was no further ahead. I did not feel seen, felt, or heard in the slightest. I didn't have words for it at the time, but the heaviness I felt energetically was palpable.

Intuitively, the moment I held my niece for the first time, I decided that I would do everything within my power to become pregnant. I instinctively fueled my body and let go of my self-destructive habits. I began to exercise, eat healthier, and take supplements to support my body. I was put on the waitlist to go and see the fertility clinic. It took me months to make that decision – waiting in limbo. I knew that going down this road was going to reap reward or heartache. I also instinctively knew that if I put everything within my control and grasp into it and if it brought nothing at the end of it, I would know that I tried everything humanly possible to make it happen. That I would have no regrets because I had left no stone unturned.

The entire fertility treatment process felt like an out-of-body experience. I felt completely disconnected from my body and did not enjoy the side effects. When I got my period, not only was I beyond sad and disappointed, but they were excruciatingly painful. The surge of hormones and all that I was subjecting myself to was wreaking havoc on my mind and body. I would call in sick for work and lie in a fetal position in my bed. I would give myself one day, and that was it. That was all I allowed myself to sit and feel sorry for myself, and then I would continue on like nothing had happened. From the exterior, nothing was visible, but on the inside, the continual loss was taking a toll on my well-being.

I put so much pressure on myself and my relationship because my husband had been checked out, and the issue didn't lie with him; it was on me. Whether or not we became parents weighed so heavily on my shoulders because it was all my fault if this didn't work. But it had to – there were no other options in my mind. The amount of stress I felt to time everything correctly felt so unnatural and regimented and like we were going through the motions a lot of the time. Wasn't this supposed to be a fun process? Not an all-consuming life-altering stage of life? In theory, we had 'time', but this was taking so much time and energy, and we could walk away empty-handed.

After years of trying, we finally got a positive pregnancy test. I couldn't believe it! It had finally happened. We went to the fertility clinic, and when I was asked what I saw, I said 'two' and asked what the doctor saw. TWINS – we were having twins! I was so grateful to be blessed with not one; but two.

Even though I was thrilled, I never celebrated my pregnancy properly. It had taken so long to conceive that I was scared that now that I had them, I would lose them. I wouldn't leave the city or let anyone throw me a baby shower because loss was wired in my nervous system. I couldn't allow myself to feel joy because if I was too happy, that would be the moment that it would all be taken away.

Despite having a successful pregnancy and two bundles of joy at home, a part of me always wondered why my infertility had been unexplained. I told myself to just be thankful that I got two because some people do not get to have one baby, let alone two. I tried to silence the voice that questioned what was wrong with me. Why couldn't I conceive naturally? Why didn't the doctors have any answers for me?

With what I now know, I can truly credit my twins to mindset, prioritizing my nutrition and exercising, quitting a stressful job, the love I have for my husband, and fertility drugs. I left the clinic after being told that it should have worked by now and that they were going to investigate further. I felt utterly deflated because I had been doing and trying everything to an exact science, and it hadn't reaped any results. I felt like a failure as a woman. Wasn't that the one thing we were 'meant to do' on earth, and I couldn't even do that. It relieved the pressure that I was putting on myself though we were still trying but waiting for everything to go through for the next steps. When I stopped trying to force it to happen and was able to just be is when two little souls were like, pick me!

As my twins grew and were not quite as dependent on me, I began going to karma yoga classes for a bit of 'me' time and peace and quiet. Sometimes, I would go with my friend, Anna, and always felt like a brand new person afterwards. I was quickly becoming a yogi and wanted more of it in my life!

When my friend, Anna, died unexpectedly in an accident similar to my brother and step-brother's death, it really triggered me. She truly embodied living life to the fullest and followed her dancing dreams. At the bottom of my heart, I knew that I needed to find a peaceful way to handle my grief instead of letting it turn my world upside down every time it happened. Death is part of the life cycle, but it evoked such a raw and vulnerable state within that it shook me to the core of my being. It was the catalyst for me to stop waiting until the kids were older and to follow my dreams now by signing up for my first yoga teacher training. My first yoga teacher training scratched the surface of how I was unconsciously creating my own suffering in my life.

I remember crying through a hot yoga class and being front and centre looking at myself in the mirror and still not wanting to feel and process the emotions that had been stirred up within me. I was trying to contain them with every ounce of my being because I viewed crying as weak because of how my mind was programmed. Crying was only acceptable out of sight and out of mind, and you do not show your pain to the world. I was so used to holding everything in and keeping everybody out that I was beyond mortified that I could not contain myself. I was such a prisoner of my mind and when, where, and how it was acceptable to express myself. Embracing yoga was the beginning of self-acceptance of all of me, not just the pieces of me I deemed worthy.

I was still very much led astray by ego. After completing one teacher training, I signed up for another one so that I would have the knowledge to teach various styles of yoga classes. What I encountered instead was moving beyond the physical practice to what yoga truly is. I believe that initially, yogis are fascinated with the physical practice, but once they dive deeper and embody the essence of yoga in all areas of their life, not just on their yoga mat, then they are forever and irrevocably transformed into their true Self. The connection to Spirit is reignited, and they reside back into their true nature.

The Happyness Centre began to peel back the layers of who I truly was, to stop looking externally for answers and tap into my inner being. To awaken to my inner wisdom and to trust the messages being received. I learned to sit with the issues in my tissues in yin, move through discomfort in my mind and body, and connect to my Spirit, who finally was reawakened after lying dormant for all those decades. I started to love myself unconditionally instead of pursuing it from external sources, releasing the need for validation with each pose and every breath. To come home to myself in all of my glory. To be unafraid to be me and to stop dimming my light for other people.

I had lived a fiery yang lifestyle for so long, but it was my yin training when I began to notice the energetic shifts occurring within me. I began to feel more at ease in my body. This transitioned into learning the restorative practice and is truly what allowed my mind and body to release the grip the past had over it and finally make peace with it. To no longer be the victim in my life because the only person that I was hurting was myself. To fully surrender to the realization that I had unconsciously been creating loss in my life and to heal those parts of me that needed healing. When the light of awareness was shone that I had almost denied myself from the very thing I wanted most in my life, it gave me so much pause and was the most significant 'aha' moment of my life. I felt decades of emotions released from my body that had been leaving no room for anything else to grow. When you release what no longer serves you, there is space for new creation. In a moment of passion, desire, and love, I wished a baby could be created, and it was. I broke through the limiting belief that I needed to use a fertility clinic in order to conceive. I did not. I healed and cleared my sacral chakra and my "Buddha baby" manifested. I had an easy pregnancy, a natural delivery (I was hiking when my water broke because I wanted this baby to come out on its own!) I was so tuned in and connected with him and his cues once he was in my arms and we were at baby + me yoga at 10 days old. I was confident and competent and trusted myself and my journey.

The key to transformation was being given the knowledge and applying what I had learned on my mat to my day-to-day life. To notice my habitual patterns and be conscious and aware of when my mind was running the same old story and creating a new one. To become present to how and where and why I hold stress in certain parts of my body and to be able to consciously relax my nervous system. To be equipped with the resources I need in order to move myself out of fight or flight mode and back into rest and digest mode. To give my mind, body, and spirit what it needs and for that locust of control to be shifted from external to internal. I trust my intuition and the messages that my body is giving me above and beyond everything else. I know without a shadow of a doubt that I would not have conceived naturally if it were not for me restoring my trust, faith, and hope within myself. As well as letting go of all of the things that were holding me back that had become known and familiar to me energetically, but that didn't serve me. I didn't go to yoga and meditation with the intention of trying to conceive. It is what naturally happened when I became whole again – I was never broken, but I felt like it. I know precisely why I struggled the first time around and how I was able to conceive with ease the more my mind, body and spirit opened up. Moving from infertile to fertile was nurturing myself from the inside out. I know precisely why I was on my mat when I had the most enlightening moment of my life. My thoughts and energy had created my reality, but I also realized my true power and potential of working with my energetic body. The only limitations were the ones I had placed on myself. My fertility was in my own hands all along; I just had not awakened to that fact. My health and well-being were never outside of my own control, even though it felt like it was undergoing fertility treatment.

The pandemic has had its silver linings, and that has been pivoting to become an online Holistic Fertility Coach in order to help women struggling to conceive. To get to the root of their infertility by clearing their chakras by connecting with their divine feminine self to release energy blocks within and come back into balance and alignment, which is their true nature. To customize a 1:1 program that works for them and their journey to give them the supportive energy medicine they need in order to conceive naturally.

My work ripples out and touches others by giving them hope that conception is possible for them too and that they are not alone in their fertility journey. That a sacred safe space is created for them so that they can trust their body and surrender to the present moment, and release their suffering. I am following my soul's calling to walk beside those who are seeking liberation in their fertility journey and finding the missing piece within. Supporting those struggling to move from a place of darkness; to a place of illumination by accepting and surrendering to all that is and is meant to be. These ancient practices have existed for so long for a reason, as your light shines brightly to guide the way back to your true Self - your inner essence. It was never outside of you – it was inside of you all along, awaiting illumination.

ABOUT THE AUTHOR

ASHLEY HOLMES

Ashley Holmes is the Founder of Holistic Fertility Coach Inc., RYT 200 Hatha Yoga, RYT 300 Yin, Kriya, Restorative & Therapeutic Yoga, Meditation Guide, Ayurvedic health and wellness educator, Reiki Second Degree & Published Author. Her passion for customizing yoga, meditation, chakras, Ayurveda & Reiki empowers women to come back into balance and alignment to heal themselves and conceive with ease. She uses this energy medicine to support women struggling with infertility to help them conceive naturally by healing their sacral chakra. She strives to help as many women as humanly possible to restore their trust and faith in their bodies to fulfill their baby dreams. She believes this is the best gift to give someone and is honored to help those seeking to not walk this path alone. She resides in British Columbia with her husband, twins, and miracle baby.

Facebook:
https://www.facebook.com/ashley.holmes3979
Facebook Group:

https://www.facebook.com/groups/271957647919481
Instagram:
https://www.instagram.com/ashley_holmes3202/
Email:
yogaforfertility7@gmail.com

DAVID ALISON

TIME, POSSIBILITIES, AND CHANGE

*L*ooking across the bay to the mist-covered hills on the Isle of Mull, my thoughts and memories dance together like the raindrops in front of me that are blown across the window. As I write this, we are in the last days of December 2021, and as the year ends, I sit here in gratitude for several things.

Firstly, I am still alive. I recently had an unexpected spell in hospital with a very serious infection in my lungs, diagnosed as C19. Unexpected as I am a very healthy, fit hiker and 60-year-old biker. Being told on admission by the consultant that it was "touch and go" and the next 48 hours were crucial came as a complete shock. After 7 days in a hospital bed on an oxygen feed and IV-fed medications, I was strong enough to leave the hospital, and 3 weeks later, I sit here on the Sacred Island of Iona in Scotland writing the words that you are reading.

Secondly, I now have a deeper sense of the sacredness and sanctity of this beautiful gift we all share. What is this gift? You may be asking; it is the gift of life. Having been close to death only a matter of weeks ago, I am reminded that we never really know what lies in front of us and that I, for one, will spend the rest of my life in alignment with my values and passions, finding joy and fulfillment in everything I do.

Thirdly, for having the opportunity to share my story with you, it is my desire to encourage and inspire you to become the man or woman you were born to be. To find in the words of the M People song "Search for the Hero" and the key to you living a soul-led life.

Where and when did this all start for me? I turn the clock back and the hands of time to 1977. I had just left further education college after 8 months of attempting to add to the 2 basic qualifications I left school with. I lived in Glasgow in the suburbs, my father was a civil servant, my mother was a part-time Nursing Auxiliary, and I grew up in a religious home. My parents and grandparents had strong Christian beliefs and were leaders in the local Baptist church. I had a comfortable life at home, my meals were cooked, my clothes washed, and I had clean sheets on my bed every week.

1977 living in Scotland was tough, unemployment was high, and the traditional manual industries of shipbuilding and mining were in decline. It was no surprise therefore that I spent several months with no job. I had no real idea of what I wanted to do; I did not have the qualifications to go to university, not that I had ever studied; my exam passes to date had been marginal passes that came from memory.

My dream as a boy growing up in a football-mad city was to be a professional footballer. That dream ended when as a 12-year-old, my football development stopped when the local boys club U13 league started playing on a Sunday. As my father pointed out to me, Sunday was God's Day and not a day for playing football; therefore, I could not continue playing football at this level. He shared the story of Eric Liddell, a famous Scottish Rugby Player and Athlete who famously refused to run in the 100-yard heats in the 1924 Olympics as they were on a Sunday; the 1980s movie Chariots of Fire tells his story. I was crushed and spent my senior school years as my teachers would say, "a bright boy but is a dreamer who doesn't apply himself."

After 4 months, I got a job as a Trainee Manager in the biggest superstore in Scotland, which was 2 miles from where I lived. This lasted around a week when, after an incident in the department I worked in, I was called to the manager's office to be told I would never make a manager and was demoted to the trolley guy, collecting the customers' trolleys from the car park. Going home as an upset naïve boy, my father's advice was to "prove him wrong," which I went on to do well into my fifties, despite getting my first managerial position at the age of 19.

Looking back at this experience now, the emotions I felt gave me hunger and drive to prove myself and a desire to succeed. I went on to become a Supply Chain Professional working in many functions and industries. I also got a university education, obtaining a Masters Degree from a leading Business School in the UK, coming in the top third in my class. My Ego was in its element, driving my thoughts, emotions, and actions. I always found myself in roles where I could be seen to make a difference; there were always situations that needed to be improved; I was the man to fix them, by fixing them, I felt good enough, when I achieved results, I was respected. I felt worthy.

The dark side of this hunger and drive was that I was subconsciously driven by fear, and that voice inside my head said, "you will be found out" or "you are not good enough" which I now know are the elements of Imposter Syndrome. On many occasions, it would end up saying "told you so". This played out across my corporate career with repeated patterns of success, then perceived failure as projects ended, roles were made redundant, or I was fired. However, the Ego was still running the show as each time I started a new position, I earned more money, had a higher status, and was given more responsibility. My response to this was to keep pushing; the more success and money I got, the more I wanted.

Push without balance will eventually wear you out

IN PARALLEL, my personal life went on a similar path of repeated patterns; Ego led behaviours, thoughts, emotions, and actions. In my mid-teens, I was quiet; I had no real confidence with women, my main interests were music, motorbikes, and football. In the circles I frequented, none of the young women I liked were interested in me.

I had my first serious relationship when I was 19, and we went on to get married and have two beautiful daughters. Our marriage ended in 1997; we had been together 18 years. A few years later, my next serious relationship was with someone much younger than me, which lasted 18 months. In 2002, I then had a 2-year relationship with a Frenchwoman and then met my second wife a few years later. We got divorced at the end of 2011.

The common thread in each of these relationships was that I had attracted women who had all been through difficult life experiences, parental abuse, drug addiction, bulimia, depression, and domestic violence. My Ego in the form of the white knight, just like in my professional career, was that I could be the saviour and "fix" the situation. In most cases and in some of my subsequent relationships, I would become a people pleaser, doing everything I could to make them happy, feel loved and secure. My belief was that in doing this, I would be wanted, loved, desired, respected, and happy. I had given the power to my emotions away and couldn't see it, and the fact that only they had the power to change their emotions.

In late 2011, I moved from England to Amsterdam on a 3-month contract which ended up being a 2.5 year salaried position. I had just divorced from my second wife and was at my lowest point emotionally and mentally. I had the support of a counsellor back in the UK, and I started looking for the answers to life in 2 directions, one was in reading spiritual books, the first was "The Pilgrimage" by Paulo Coelho, the other path was throwing myself into the thriving expat culture in Amsterdam. The second path was the one that my Ego enjoyed most, and it soon took over a large part of my life.

I would spend at least 3 nights a week out drinking or at parties with ever-increasing quantities of alcohol being consumed. I was becoming addicted.

When my contract ended, I started freelancing and quickly got myself a role working in 2 countries for a multimedia company, and the travel reduced my ability and dependency on my Amsterdam vibe.

Then in late 2014, the universe stepped in, and after a serendipitous exchange with a headhunter in the USA, I found myself being invited for the dream job that I had envisioned in 2003. In January 2015, I started a job as Operations Director for an American Fortune 500 company with 5 departments, 800 staff in 8 countries and a $100m budget based in Antwerp, Belgium, with the largest salary package of my career.

Looking back on the steps of my career and in my personal life, I can now say from experience and insight that everything happens in divine timing, opportunities are created, and if you listen to your intuition, instinct or Ego, you will take a path. That path will lead you to either lessons or blessings. I have so many examples of this in both my personal and professional life.

Four months into driving my dream job, the wheels started to loosen. A serious Health & Safety incident meant I had to make decisions that would protect the workforce; however, they started a series of events that highlighted the weaknesses in the structure and processes across the company. Over the next 2 years, there were many changes, not least my 3 bosses in 18 months. Every week brought new challenges, more boardroom conflict and increasing pressure from international headquarters.

I was heading for burnout; the constant demands on travel, operational challenges, key staff leaving or having to be replaced was taking its toll. I was constantly living in fear of the next problem; the boardroom politics drained me. Each new boss wanted something a little different. I sat many nights asking the question, "Is this really what life is about? Have I done all this to live a life of stress and anxiety, is it the price of my private enjoyment?

My alternate path of spirituality was becoming more prominent in my life; I stopped returning to Amsterdam for the expat scene, read more, and watched more informational documentaries and talks than binging on TV series. Then one Friday, everything changed. I was in my apartment scrolling through social media on my phone and got a message to watch a documentary by a famous Personal Development Expert; that documentary was "I Am Not Your Guru", and it changed my life. I watched it 5 times, each time it reduced me to tears. In meditation, I asked what do I need to know? I then visualised and saw myself coaching, speaking, healing and having a completely different quality of life

Everything changed from that point; I hired a personal and spiritual coach. Within 3 months, I invested and started coach training at a leading coach training school in Brussels. In our first call, my spiritual coach confirmed she also saw what I had foreseen and told me I would work for one of the biggest personal development organisations in the world.

In August 2017, I came back from my first personal development event in New York, pumped up and inspired, ready to take on my corporate challenges with new vigour. Then the universe stepped in. Sometimes in life, your timing is not what is in the plan. 20 minutes into my first day at the office, I was called to a meeting where I was fired and marched out of the building with no opportunity to say goodbye to any of my team.

In September 2017, at the age of 55, I started my new career and coaching business. By the end of the year, I had successfully completed an intensive 3-month process to secure a contract as an international coach for that same company as predicted by my spiritual coach. In January 2018 I successfully completed my training at coach school.

I was now dancing in two places in my mind; I felt the call from the universe, I answered it, the alignment of my dream job ending and my first contract for my coaching business, and on the other side that little voice, Who are you to be coaching? How will you make money?

The Universe always has your back whichever path you walk

2018 BEGAN in a completely new vibration, a 180-degree change in my career, the 35 years of corporate management experience began slowly melting into the memory banks of my body and mind. Each day began with meditation, frequently some exercise, and then preparation for the coaching calls of that day. Gone were the early morning red-eye flights, the constant meetings, and problem solving, the stress and pressure. I was 6 months into a relationship with a woman with whom I could just be me, no need to "fix" anything, just enjoy being present; I was happy and excited for the future. I was in control of my time, my energy, and it felt like my life. The year went quickly, and before I knew it, I was celebrating Christmas.

My competence as a coach had grown exponentially; I was coaching 5 days a week, some months completing over 150 sessions. My clients were getting great results. What I hadn't noticed, however, was that I was falling into old patterns, my working hours became longer, and I began to sacrifice my own personal time. The contract I had with the personal development organisation had many benefits; the support and peer community were good; I travelled across Europe to support events; however, the financial compensation was low, and I had to do a lot of sessions and back up with sales commissions to support my living costs in Belgium. Growing my private business was also proving a challenge due to my energy levels, and my small apartment began to feel claustrophobic being there day and night most weeks. I knew that for 2019 things would have to change. The universe again stepped in and gave me options

As the first quarter of 2019 passed, I noticed that in my coaching, I was becoming more and more intuitive, tapping into newfound talents, and learning to trust my intuition more, and my coaching became more fluid and spirit led. It was becoming more transparent that living in Belgium, where a combination of Language (English is the 3rd spoken language) and high taxes would not be sustainable moving forward.

In early April, my girlfriend called me and said she needed to talk, and she would come over the following night. I instinctively knew the topic of discussion. That night as I meditated, I had a clear message and vision that it was now time for me to go home, back to Scotland after 32 years. The next phase of my life would begin there. The next night, we shared what was in our hearts, and we agreed on a path forward.

I returned to Scotland in June 2019 and after some "tests" from the universe, I settled in a beautiful farmhouse in southern Scotland in the countryside at the edge of a small village. I had space to live, a fantastic office with beautiful vista from the windows, I could hold small events, and it was close to some great hiking and biking routes. Following my soul's calling, I had been given a new lease of life.

Almost immediately, events started to happen that led to me finding a business mentor in Scotland, who, as it turned out, lived 20 minutes from my home. We put together a plan which would see me do further training in NLP and Hypnotherapy, become a speaker, hold my own events, and launch my first program in 2020.

In February 2020, I made my first speaking engagement in front of 450 people in Glasgow, opening my mentor's flagship event. It felt like home; my years of experience speaking to teams from my corporate career combined with my ever-deepening spiritual awareness made it effortless.

My first event was booked for March, and I was feeling excited and passionate about the future. I would soon be able to end my agreement with the personal development company and take my business in a new direction. Then the world changed completely, the whole world, not just my world.

This led me to push even harder; I signed more private clients and invested in a new peer group, a Mastermind. The old patterns began creeping in again, I took on more work with the personal development company, started a bespoke Business Coaching opportunity, and very soon, I was back in the long hour's cycle, taking on too much, feeling the need to prove myself, I could not stop, the voices in my head came back strong, and I was in constant push mode.

My spiritual coach in one of our sessions at the time told me that she was getting messages that I had to be more of Human BE-ing rather than DO-ing; this was not the first time in our 5 years of working together that she had shared this. I was juggling with priorities and kept pushing to give my best to the different areas of my business. In most of them, I was finding resistance from my own internal thoughts and external sources; it was beginning to become an energy

38

drain. Very shortly after this, the Universe stepped in again, this time in quite a dramatic way.

My eldest daughter came to stay with me for my birthday week; I took her on her first hike up a Scottish Mountain on my birthday. It was a beautiful day; both of us connected in nature despite the mist and rain. I frequently hike in the Scottish mountains and get to the peaks; sometimes, along paths that require courage and concentration, it's part of my adventure DNA, along with riding my large motorcycle.

At the weekend, we took a walk down to the village and through the woods, then down a small slope to walk along the banks of the River Clyde. It was an easy walk I had done hundreds of times, this time; however, as I reached the base of the slope, within a second, I had slipped and landed on my side with my elbow going into my ribs. I could not breathe, my daughter ran over and helped me sit up, and I slowly managed to regain my breath. The pain was excruciating, and following a visit to the hospital, it was confirmed I had broken 4 ribs.

Sleeping and sitting became a challenge; luckily, I have an electric desk that allows me to work standing up, so I could keep coaching. Any other activity was not possible, and it took all my energy to manage the calls that had been scheduled. My commitments had to be prioritised, and I had to listen to my body and slow down so that I could recover. Slowing down brought me to a place where I had time, albeit enforced, to stop and listen. In this period, I had a clear vision that I would manifest my highest bank balance in the business at the end of the year, end my agreement with the personal development company, and start working on a homeless project concept for people in Scotland. By the end of January 2021, they had all happened.

Soul aligned actions & learning to surrender will manifest your desires

2021 BROUGHT me closer on the scale to surrender and further from push as the year progressed, I brought in the most revenue in my 4 years as a coach, I had a concept to create rehabilitation for homeless people in Scotland. Then the universe stepped in again, and I was hospitalised with a life-threatening illness.

In reflection of my life journey since those days, I have this strong feeling that there has been a reset; my comfort levels in following my soul's calling are now much wider. I know that there is more to come for me; the next chapter of my life is beginning, my soul will create the adventures. My belief in divine timing confirmed.

Love, Light and Blessings to YOU all

ABOUT THE AUTHOR

DAVID ALISON

David Alison is the Founder of David Alison Coaching. Leaving school at 15 with no significant qualifications, he was told by his first Manager that he would never make it in Management. He went on to achieve a Master's degree at the renowned Cranfield University Business School in 2002, and a board-level position in a Fortune 500 company based in Europe in 2015.

In 2016 he made the soul-led decision to make a complete career change and become a Transformational coach. After becoming a Certified Coach in 2017, he started his Coaching & Therapy Business, completing over 4300 sessions in the last 4 years. His work guides Business Owners & Leaders to find purpose and fulfillment through transforming their Life & Business.

He wants to see a world where everyone could lead a soul-led life of possibilities, unlimited potential, passion, and fulfillment.

LinkedIn:
https://www.linkedin.com/in/davidalison/
Instagram:

https://www.instagram.com/davidalisoncoaching/
Website:
https://www.davidgalison.com/
Facebook:
https://www.facebook.com/groups/261569322147441

DENISE SARACCO-ZOPPI

FEAR: DREAM KILLER OR DREAM MAKER?

*I*t was September 7, 2011 when I found myself singing to the Full Moon rising in the evening sky. I was in the middle of an Ayahuasca Ceremony in Peru, and I was experiencing the bliss of Oneness with the Sacred. Prophetic messages and soulful awakenings were received this night. I decided to fully embrace this fleeting moment. I stepped outside briefly to experience nature from my heightened bliss state. I sang my heart into Grandmother Moon that night, and it was almost as if she drew nearer to me, singing back to me, and held me in her silvery moon rays. More bliss. It was like being held by the Goddess Herself. I was completely overtaken by how loved I am by All Beings.

I returned back to the Maloca Temple, about to walk inside, and as I placed my hand on the doorknob, I was immediately struck by a moment requiring a decision. Before my eyes flashed memories of the past 4 years that Mama Ayahuasca called me to sit with Her. All those years, the experiences, the deep soulful callings, the doubts and insecurities, everything came flooding back, but now with a question. "This is the moment I have called you for. Will you take more of the Yage and see what I have truly planned for you this night?"

Even in my bliss state, I knew to ingest more of the Ayahuasca Medicine would thrust me into a far deeper experience. I knew my bliss would not follow me there either. I didn't know what exactly Mama Ayahuasca had planned for me, but it clearly required my consent and more psychoactive medicine to pull it out.

Fear.

* * *

Do I take the next step? Am I ready for a big change? Is it time for me to move in a completely different direction? Will I ever have a baby? Is there a better job for me out there? Will I ever find Mr. or Mrs. Right? When will it be MY TIME to live MY LIFE?

Fear.

How you consciously move through the gates of fear will determine your outcome. That's right. How YOU consciously move determines your outcome.

You see, fear is simply an agent of change. A teacher. A trickster. Fear presents you with the opportunity to experience Truth. How you wield Fear Medicine in your life can either keep you frozen, stuck, blocked, and living a dead life – or – liberate you into a wild, free, unknown, living your fullest and best life.

That choice is always yours to make. And you don't make it just once. Oh no. Fear asks you to make that decision daily, hourly, sometimes moment after moment. Because when you walk with Fear, She will never leave you until you're through Her realms of illusions, shadows, and the great unknown. And that is perhaps the most terrifying and yet comforting thing about Fear. She's there until you learn Her lessons. And when you've embraced Her lessons, She departs until She's needed again, or until you ask for Her presence to be near. She is the comfort, the guide, the illusion-stripper, the reality-maker. She is known by many names from nearly every indigenous culture. In my tradition, she is Bone Mother. Bone Mother has been a part of my life from the very beginning. Her direct, grounded, no-nonsense wisdom has been foundational in my life right away since birth.

I am the daughter born of a strong-willed, independent, philanthropic Mom. My Mom was born of my fierce Nana, who raised her 4 children as a single mother back in the 1950's; an era when this was no small feat. Instilled in my Mom was the sheer will to thrive despite the odds stacked against her. Taking on 2 or 3 jobs to provide for the family, my Mom learned at a young age that life is what you make of it, and to never be a victim. Mom was choosy in her marital partners and found the strength she admired within herself reflected within my Father. Together, they became a torrential force that sustained us all through some great difficulties.

These teachings flowed down to my sister and me to help make us strong against a sometimes cruel world. We were taught to work through our fears, even as little girls. And Mom was an excellent guide in this. I definitely didn't like the coarse way she taught me resiliency, but she was very effective. Through the many apprehensions I had as a young child, Mom always found a way to help me face the things I feared and realize it wasn't as scary as I was making it out to be in my mind.

Early on, we all had to face the fear of my grand mal seizures. Those seizures were the scary kind: the ones where I stopped breathing during convulsions. My parents took me to the best doctors in New York City, only to be given quasi answers that didn't help. Because the seizures were few in total, I had no true seizure disorder. The doctors simply thought one side of my brain was developing faster than the other.

Mom didn't stop there. She focused her efforts on natural ways to heal me through diet, and helped me to have a plan when I felt a seizure coming on, no matter where I was. This plan ended up being most effective.

For me, those seizures were something "else". On the outside, I was dying during the seizure. For me, however, I experienced non-ordinary reality beings and lands. I remember during my first seizure, around the age of two, I was taught how to connect with the spiritual realms by simply shifting my consciousness. I remember clicking my consciousness on and off from those realms during the seizure. Upon return to my physical body, my body stabilized and returned to normal – like nothing ever happened. It was just a few moments in Earth time, but for me, I was gone for what felt like a few hours.

Throughout my childhood until around the age of eighteen, I connected with the spirit realms often; totaling about three years in the spirit world by this age. During those experiences, I was taught how to heal, do magic, and defend myself and others. I became a Doctor, a Magician, and a Warrior.

Little did I realize at the age of eighteen that all these experiences would shape my sacred calling. I thought all of it was made up of childish fantasies, and that it was time to get serious about my real life. I decided to stop connecting with the spirit worlds, and instead pursue "an adult life". I set my sights on college and beginning my ordinary world life. I always wanted to be a Doctor, but I couldn't decide if I wanted to be a Veterinarian, an Optometrist, or a Psychotherapist. I took jobs and classes in each of these fields, and I just loved it all. This began my adult walk with Fear. I was afraid of choosing the wrong path. I walked with much doubt at this time as well. I was unsure how I would forge my path, life, and destiny in this world. I decided to pursue boring Business, because my parents knew I could land a great job with that degree. And they were right! I landed my first job as an Admin for a non-profit organization and quickly moved up to Executive Secretary within six months. This was the time I met my first "wake up" call from the Sacred.

I took a person with disabilities with a seizure disorder to the hospital after she had a seizure in front of me. This was standard protocol. What happened in that ER room, I never expected. I began having my own pre-seizure signs and ended up having a grand mal seizure right there. My soul went up into the Heavens, and there was a party welcoming my return. This place was similar to the places I've visited in the spirit world before, but this time was different. There was so much love, peace, and light in this place. I was Home. This was the place I belonged, and I had zero issues if my physical body died fully. I was enjoying my time with hundreds of angelic and celestial beings when one of them pulled me aside. He was a handsome angel with salt and pepper hair, amazingly bright, calm blue eyes, and a smile of peaceful contentment that just made me feel immediately relaxed.

"It's time to return now. You have many important things to do." He told me. I was shocked. I really thought I was going to stay and enjoy my Home here. Frantically, I began exclaiming, "I don't want to go back!" over and over and over.

Suddenly, BOOM. There I was. In the hospital. The nurses gave me smelling salts to help me to wake up. Despite being very bright, it felt very dark compared to where I'd just come from. I felt the sadness, the heaviness, and the sickness of this world. It hit me like a ton of bricks. My spirit was so disheartened and disappointed to be here. And that began a period of new Fear that initiated me into my Sacred Calling.

Over the next several months, little by little, I was having "symptoms". I felt entirely disconnected from my body; like I was a space cadet trying to find the mechanism to ground on the floor of this reality but unable to. My eyes immediately became hyper-sensitive to light right after the seizure. I began experiencing headaches, migraines, and it all escalated to where I couldn't lift my head off my pillow in the morning without severe dizziness. I was scared. What was wrong with me?

Good 'ole Mom to the rescue...again...taking me to the best doctors to try to figure out a diagnosis and cure. I had nicknamed it the "Denise Disease" when all of the tests came back as "normal". I was back to where I was as a little girl: scared, being a pin cushion, and afraid of all these medical procedures. It was really bad DeJa'Vu. I fell into a place of despair. I didn't know how to help myself. I was sick and yet the doctors didn't believe me. I was on disability from work, and my quality of life was very poor due to all the limitations I had.

One night, I felt a literal explosion go off in my head. It scared the crap out of me! I woke up startled, but with a strong knowing. I immediately knew that I was off my life path, and my healing would begin when I return to my roots, heal myself with what I knew how to do, and lean on my amazing family to help me beat the "Denise Disease".

That next day, I organized for a one-week stay at my parents' house just to make sure this was the right thing to do. That one week helped me to see that I needed to take charge of my health and wellness. I was convinced that if I was healthy, my aligned path would find me.

...and it did.

For seven years I battled the "Denise Disease". I was able to desensitize my fear responses enough to halfway handle ordinary reality. I landed a new job as a temp and was hired full-time. I was earning enough money to move out again, but I was still not right. I was still battling depression. I still didn't want to "be here". It haunted me badly. I sought professional help, but it wasn't even close to what I needed.

I began accepting that this ordinary life of my 9-5 job was good enough for me. After all, it afforded me the physical world success I was looking for. I was excellent at my job, and I kept being promoted. But I was bored to tears. I tried every day to find something I enjoyed about that job and focused on that. Alas, the Sacred had something else in mind for me...

After receiving Reiki for the first time during a massage, something inside me woke up. Something inside me turned on. For seven nights thereafter, at exactly 11:11pm, I would experience these energetic waves of energy. My body was paralyzed and I was so scared. It would last about a half-hour as these energy surges danced up and down my body. The angelic guide who forced me back to my body came through during this time, and reassured me everything was ok, that I was being "tuned up".

After my "tune-ups" finished, I was suddenly able to hear Spirit like I used to as a child. Suddenly, I was receiving audible guidance so strongly it was as if someone was physically next to my ear speaking to me. And more than once, that guidance saved me from a car crash and other accidents.

This was such an undeniable sign that I was called to reconnect with the Sacred, that I immediately began my practices in Meditation, Music, Yoga, and seeking out apprenticeship opportunities. It didn't take long for me to realize that all my experiences in the Spirit World were, in fact, REAL. I had never once considered them to be real. I thought I made up the whole thing in this fantastical, whimsical way so I could escape the pressures of life each night and have these wild experiences! My teachings and guidance from the Spirit World led me to learn about nature, magic, and quickly led me to my first Shamanic Apprenticeship. I felt like I returned to a state of being I had known as a child. I began waking up parts of my soul that I deemed childish and unacceptable. My sacred gifts were open, and I was well on my way to making some huge inner shifts. I started to feel "awake" vs on autopilot in my life.

About halfway through my apprenticeship, I realized one day I've made a full recovery of the "Denise Disease" physical symptoms! I hadn't noticed that physical reality was much easier to manage. The suffering of my mind, heart and soul was next. I still carried much ache in my spirit of wanting to be a spirit myself and return Home. Not a single person was able to help me heal this, and despite my amazing spiritual guidance and healing tools, I was not able to find that way on my own. I was tired of living like a ghost. I was tired of suffering. I was desperate and ready to do whatever I needed to do to heal that ache. And after 4 years of being in Ceremony with Mama Ayahuasca in dreamtime, feeling Her call in my soul so strongly, I felt this was the Sacred pointing me in the healing direction I needed.

BACK IN PERU, with my hand on the doorknob, Mama Ayahuasca asked me if I was ready to, essentially, overdose on the Yage to deepen my experience. After all, it was this moment that she called me for… and She needed my full conscious consent. Fear. Will I die? Many others have died by overdosing on the Ayahuasca Yage. Will this happen to me too?

I have this rule when it comes to how I'm feeling called by the

Spirit: SAY YES. No matter how much fear I may feel in the Yes, I do it anyways. Maybe it's FOMO. Maybe I'm really crazy or really dumb. Inside me, my truth is that I'm a warrior who refuses to allow FEAR to rule her life.

I stepped into the Maloca Temple, went up to the altar, ingested my second dose, and 10 minutes later, the whole reason for my being there was revealed.

What appeared before me was a cold, stone slab in the middle of Machu Picchu. I knew this slab all too well. I read about it many times. It is the Altar of Death.

"Sacrifice your life upon the Altar of Death," Mama Ayahuasca commanded.

I learned that night that there are some things you cannot escape no matter how much it scares you. Death is one of those things. I fought with Fear the entire rest of the night. I was in my microcosmic experience trying to let go and die, but Death has its own time, and frankly, it took waaaaay too long for me. I had to surrender to my inevitable Death, in Death's time. I said goodbye to my life, hopes, unfinished dreams, and fears. I spoke to each beloved family member and friend in spirit this night and said my goodbyes. During the Ceremony, I turned to a gentleman and asked him to take care of my physical body when I die and to bring me to my parents. He agreed, and that set me at ease.

Ceremony ended. Everyone went to their respective rooms to sleep for a few hours. I was left alone in the dark, cold Maloca Temple, laying on the floor, urinating myself repeatedly. And just like that, without any dignity or fanfare or anyone by my side, I died. I crossed through the Eye of God and arrived at the point of no return. I was given a choice: reclaim my life and my sacred calling or continue with death and cross over completely.

Roaring through me came my highest self, represented as a Jaguar. She came from deep within my soul, bounding forward with fervor, and like the rumble of thunder, She/I declared life. I had no idea that I embodied the Medicine of Life Itself. There was no choice. "Life is Sacred" and every ounce of life was claimed.

This time, I CHOSE to be here in this life. I was not forced back into my body. Since embracing Fear this night, I have never been haunted by "not wanting to be here" again. To think that if I had listened to Fear, I wouldn't have had the experience I needed to heal that lost part of my soul.

* * *

YOU SEE, the other side of Fear is Evolution. If you have the courage to walk beside your Fear, through the shadows of your mind, through the land of illusions and bone, you'll eventually transition into a whole new world, and a whole new YOU. The bigger the Fear, the bigger the rewards. Every time.

When fellow entrepreneurs ask me how I got started, I tell them it's been a lifelong journey. And there are many times when we are faced with Fear. Fear is often vilified and made into something dark. I continue to walk with Fear, and while I'm still scared, I always say "Yes" to myself and the Sacred no matter how scared I am.

In doing so, and especially since that night in Peru, my whole life has changed. I was reawakened to my Dharma. I remembered who I am and what I'm here to Be. I ended up marrying my soulmate, Joshua, another co-author in this very book, and we have a beautiful life walking our Sacred Dance together. I am full-time inside our Wellness Center, serving my sacred calling everyday. Today I have earned the blessing of living my childhood experiences in the spirit world, now manifested in physical reality. I am a Soul Doctor, a High Priestess, and a Warrior of Truth. It has been my life's journey to bring me to where I am today. The best part: that boring Business degree also has a place in my life when I'm wearing my Business hat!

It's not that I wasn't afraid millions of times. I was everytime! I risked everything - including the life I had. And I gained everything - including the life I thought was just a fantasy. No, you don't have to risk your life to make your dreams a reality. You just have to be willing to sacrifice your Fears, enter the unknown, and rediscover who you are and what you're really made of.

Fear is the opportunity to make a big change. And if you can embrace that Fear, and move through the land of shadows, illusions, and bone, you will inevitably be led back to your Sacred Path. And if you are really far off your path like I was, keep embracing Fear as the Dream Maker, and see for yourself how you and Fear can make your dreams a reality. Then Trust, take a deep breath, and Step Forward.

ABOUT THE AUTHOR

DENISE SARACCO-ZOPPI

Rev. Denise Saracco-Zoppi is CEO and Founder of Ayni Healing Arts Center, a Master Massage Therapist, "The Soul Doctor," Author, Success Coach, Shaman Mentor, and Master Ceremonialist.

Since 2006, Denise's walk with The Sacred has helped thousands of people to reclaim their wellness, sing back their souls from trauma, and alchemize their pain into purpose. She employs an intuitive holistic fusion of massage, energy healing, sound therapy, LOVE, sacred teachings, and Spirit Medicine to help her clients align with their best possible lives!

Denise and her BeLoved husband, Joshua, also own Ayni Sacred Mysteries School. They are honored to support their students' actualization and alignment of their sacred calling and dharma.

Ayni lives right in the Heart of Newton, NJ. Together, Denise, Joshua, and their therapy dog, Mama Mango, have created a sacred space for All Beings.

Website:
   https://Aynihealingartscenter.com
   Facebook:
   https://www.facebook.com/aynihealingartscenter
   Instagram:
   https://www.instagram.com/aynihealingartscenter
   Email:
   aynihealingartscenter@gmail.com
   Phone:
   862-268-3213

EZGI DEVI

BLOOMING FROM CRACKS

*A*ddiction is a hard type of conditioning to detect and acknowledge because it has so many different versions and facets. The sneakiest and the most neglected version of addiction is codependency, although it is one of the most common. Codependency is the addiction of people-pleasing to gain the love and validation from others that you cannot provide yourself. It took me a long time to address that I've been suffering from codependency. Here is the story of how I broke my codependency pattern and started to build heart-centered, conscious, and healthy relationships.

I lived most of my life in Istanbul, Turkey. There is a deep, suppressed feminine wound in my country because the nation has been governed by masculine energy for so long. Women, in general, have to work more to claim their power, worth, and freedom. That's why I've been raised to be a strong and financially free woman to have a comfortable life in Turkey. My parents are both teachers, and as educators in a middle eastern country, they witnessed a lot of suffering caused by the lack of education and scarcity. So they made sure that my brother and I were well educated to have a financially stable life. Eventually, I studied management information systems and became a software engineer. When I turned 21 years old, I got a regular job and lived by myself, financially independent and content.

At that point, all I wanted from life was a promising career, marriage, and kids. In a very short time, I started to take big steps towards success in my career. And now it was time to accomplish the next thing on my achievement list. When I turned 23, I fell in love with a narcissist and found myself in a physically and emotionally abusive, toxic relationship. I was so in love that whatever he did was acceptable to me as long as he was with me. I tolerated all the offensive and disrespectful things he said, such as "Why are you wearing a skirt? Are you trying to show your legs to men?", "You're already pretty; why are you wearing makeup?", "Why are you laughing so loud? Are you trying to get attention?", "Why are you talking to the waiter? Are you flirting?", "Men are disgusting, and you're a smart girl. If you dress up like this, it just means you're inviting." Still, we got engaged a couple of months after our first anniversary. I made myself believe that he was being jealous and protective because he loved me so much. And if I could prove to him that those were not my intentions, he would relieve and change in time.

But on the contrary, nothing had changed. The accusations and fights increasingly continued. After a while, I started to question every step I took. My body posture had changed, I started to stutter, I took all my boy friends out of my life, I didn't order anything if the servers were male, I couldn't talk to any other men. I started hating myself, drinking more, getting more and more depressed each day. He convinced me that I was the problem in the relationship and suggested that I seek professional support. Through some friends, I found a holistic therapist. That's how I met my first guru in life.

My therapist taught me how to meditate and do breathwork; she encouraged me to start doing yoga. Furthermore, she taught me to take accountability for my life experiences instead of playing the victim. She helped me open my eyes. I ended my unhealthy relationship, but most importantly, I promised myself not to allow anybody to treat me in the same way again. Then I got my yoga instructor certificate, started a new chapter in my life, slowly but surely came back to myself.

At the end of 2017, I took 1.5 months off from my work due to extreme stress and went to Peru. During the first ten days, I attended a yoga retreat, worked with shamans, and practiced plant medicine; then, I started to travel to other parts of the country by myself. While journaling in a hostel at the Sacred Valley, I heard a squeak from the main gate and someone walking in. I turned my gaze through the gate and suddenly started to feel butterflies in my stomach. When our eyes locked from across the backyard, I knew right away I was already in love. He slowly walked towards me and started to ask questions about the hostel. There was a familiarity in his voice; his energy was like home. He decided to stay at the hostel, and we ended up spending the last of my days in Peru together.

He asked me to stay, yet, I had to go. I got back home, in love and aching.

Part of me was grateful for finding the one; another part of me was resentful. I found the love of my life but had to leave him on the other side of the world. However, I had new plans for my life after my Ayahuasca ceremony in Peru. In the ceremony, I've been shown I was a musician, writer, and healer besides being an engineer and yoga instructor, but I had no clue what to do with all of those gifts. And I was committed to finding out. So as soon as I returned to Turkey, I started taking singing classes and studying mindfulness, Reiki, alchemy, and quantum mechanics. That is to say; I started consciously working on uncovering my true gifts. I shouldn't have let a love story from the other end of the world affect my life in Istanbul.

But my heart was telling another story. We kept in touch, and I found myself in a long-distance relationship. We were both broken and sore because of our unwilling separation. I knew this was the fairytale that I'd been waiting for. We started to talk about him coming to Istanbul. But he had financial restrictions to come and visit me. When he told me that he would save up for a few months, then buy a ticket and that he might be in Turkey at the end of the summer, I remember my heart's reproach, "How will I endure until the end of summer?" Plus, I was in a good place monetarily. Why wait? So I went ahead and got him a ticket from Lima to Istanbul, he accepted with one condition: He would send me the money when he saved enough. I said, "What's mine is yours; you can pay me back when you're here. No rush."

Even though there were things that I wasn't completely comfortable with, I didn't mention any of them in our conversations. The butterflies in my stomach came to life with every video call, and that feeling was enough for me. One day, when he read my message and did not reply, he said that he could not write back for technological reasons. Even though I knew as a software engineer that was a lie, I pretended to believe it and remained silent. I didn't want to create conflict. Our dream was to travel to Asia after spending a couple of months in Istanbul. And I was not going to bring up anything that could destroy our dreams. So I ignored all of my disturbances and started to arrange my life for his arrival. When I got my bonus, I quit my corporate job and started to wait for him to be by my side.

After months of long-distance, there he was in Istanbul in the summer of 2018. I was so excited for my "happily ever after" instead; it was a series of disappointments. We were deeply in love and so compatible when it came to arts and hobbies; however, as the days passed, I realized we were completely different from each other. I've always been an open book about my life; he was secretive. I am super social and talkative; he was so introverted and quiet. I have a luxurious taste; he was like a monk who sold all his possessions. My love language is quality time; his was physical touch. I've always been so analytical and questioned everything till my mind comprehends. I like asking questions to understand people's perspectives. But whatever I asked had triggered something in him, and he felt interrogated and judged. Through his reactions, I felt judged and rejected for being myself. We were in a constant loop of explaining ourselves, our intentions, and at the end of every conversation, both of us were left feeling blamed, unheard, and unseen. As the differences surfaced, disappointments began to mount within me.

I had expectations for him to be and act in certain ways. When those expectations were not met, I confronted him and blamed him for not doing what needed to be done. Because I could see his potential to be my ideal partner, I thought he would change into what I needed if I was patient enough and showed him the way. So I chose to hold onto the potentiality of a better future and kept compromising with my present moment again. I tried to control him so that he could be the person that I expected him to be. What I didn't realize was, essentially, I got some purple fabric and was trying to make a red dress out of it. Then I ended up feeling sad, mad, and disappointed for him not being the red fabric I needed.

On the other hand, I've been financing the relationship since he came to Istanbul. He came with a small amount of money, and I didn't make a deal out of it by trusting my savings. I had patiently waited for him to pay the ticket money back, but he never even mentioned it. When I finally asked, he told me he saved the money but lost it in gambling. When I heard it, our financial dynamic started to bother me. A part of me began to feel constantly angry at him. Still, when we decided to travel to Nepal, I purchased his tickets again.

After Istanbul, we went to Nepal and worked with Buddhists for three months. That's where all the spiritual work that I've done before came into fruition. My psychic abilities peaked, and I started to communicate with other entities and spirits such as angels, the moon, and water spirits. When I shared those extraordinary experiences with my partner, he told me he worked with so many healers in Peru and had seen no one communicating with the moon or the water spirits like me. I felt like my reality was being rejected. When I spoke about the teachings that I wanted to share with the world, he always said he didn't agree with them at all. For instance, I believe that doing shadow work is a must for rewriting the subconscious; he believed no one has to do anything; this life is just to be. Whatever I said was too much, whatever I thought was extreme for him. I started to feel like I had to hide some aspects of myself to be validated.

On the morning of the day, he proposed to me in Nepal; we had had a huge fight because of finances. He had taken money from my purse without asking me, and I felt violated and taken advantage of. I remember thinking of breaking up. But when I saw him on his knees in front of everybody, I convinced myself that all the issues we had were temporary, and I wanted to spend the rest of my life with him. I said yes even though I was burning with anger and resentment inside.

Since he was a Peruvian-American, his base was still in the States. At the end of 2018, we moved to the US and got married. Even though I had traveled to 26 countries before coming to the States, I started to feel alienated and insecure in Florida... I didn't feel as though I belonged. The only thing I felt belonged was my husband. I was deeply in love and committed to building a life with him. In the end, he was the only thing that felt familiar, felt like home. Therefore I attached myself to my husband and my husband's environment.

I found myself trying to fit into his life in Florida. I was deeply in need of his validation, hence I kept forcing myself to get along with people that I wouldn't normally choose to associate with. He would show up at our house unannounced with his family and friends, and it would be a problem when I wanted to be notified. Then I would try to please everyone to avoid conflict even though I didn't energetically resonate with them. As I kept betraying my feelings and needs, my boundaries kept being crossed, and our disagreements and fights kept growing larger each day.

One day, I had to work till 4 am, and my partner was supposed to pick me up from work since we only had one car. I received a text at 2 am saying, "I ended up in Miami and I'm not gonna make it, and my phone is about to die." It was not the first time he left me like that when I needed him, but this time he knew that I had no other option to go home since Uber was not working on my phone. I felt so abandoned for the millionth time. When I expressed my disappointment, his excuse was, "Plans change. You gotta learn how to be more spontaneous." I found myself with the ugly truth: there was no me in this relationship. It was all about him, his family, his friends, his dreams... And that night had changed everything for me.

I started to do some research on relationships. I was trying to understand why I keep attracting partners who make me feel rejected, abandoned, and unsafe. Alex Myles says, "Be cautious of connections that feel like home if home wasn't always a safe place for you!" When I read this sentence, I remember my world collapsed on my head and made me think of how home was for me...

When I was a kid, I witnessed the war in 1994 in the Southeastern Anatolia Region of Turkey. We had to spend most of our time in shelters. That was a huge trauma in my life that has damaged my bonds with the world because I didn't feel safe in it.

I also witnessed domestic violence in the family. My mind normalized chaos in relationships since I grew up in arguments and fights. On top of it, I always had to be the judge of the family and was asked who was right, mom or dad? Whoever I chose, the other one got offended and blamed me for choosing sides. I've learned not to speak my truth to avoid creating more conflict.

Plus, since my parents are teachers, I always had to be the example child. I've been criticized a lot. Whatever I've done, there was always a better way to do it. I grew up with "You should be an example; if not, how are the parents of our students going to trust us?" I had to be their proof of success, and if I wasn't, I got punished. So I learned to be what others wanted me to be.

On the other hand, my dad is a genius and very quiet man. He is so logical and doesn't express his emotions often. I can't say that I received the words of affirmation and emotional support that I needed from his side. As he is the first male role model for me, my mind was unconsciously seeking familiarity when it comes to the male image.

Then it all clicked! I've been choosing partners who would make me relive the love as the way I've learned love from the first source. When I looked into all of my romantic relationships, I realized I'd been attracted to emotionally unavailable and judgy men who reject my reality or react when I speak my truth. Furthermore, the men who feel unsafe... I figured I was addicted to chaos since I had to operate from fight or fight throughout my entire life! All of those butterflies that I felt at first sight had nothing to do with love... They were actually my central nervous system warning me about reliving my traumas.

All of this was merely the result of my subconscious programming and automated actions. I was the one who constantly judged and doubted myself, who didn't give the love and validation that I deserved to myself. I'd been giving my all and then expecting to receive love and validation from the ones who were not available for me. I was the one who created better stories for others and ended up disappointed and angry when they revealed their true stories. Because of my fear of rejection, I'd been self-sacrificing to please others, not speaking up my truth to avoid conflict, not setting healthy boundaries, instead just blaming and resenting. Fuck! I'd been repeating a pattern, and I had to break it...

I started with prioritizing my needs, setting healthy boundaries, and speaking up my truth assertively but in a loving way. Holy moly! All my relationships began cracking! My husband, parents, friends... No one seemed to like the new me! Still, I was committed to being myself unapologetically. I was awakened to the truth: If someone doesn't like me for being me, if someone doesn't honor me for honoring my needs, I don't need those people in my life anyway, right? I lost so many people along the way and me being me brought an end to my marriage.

When we split up, all the grief and pain I've been going through allowed me to birth the Wise Wild Wombmen community. I knew that going through those painful relationship experiences could guide and support so many women who go through similar experiences. My scars were also gifts that I can offer to the world. So I launched my first online course about how to understand the mind and build healthy relationships. Then started hosting women circles and events, sharing all the tools that allowed me to realize my patterns and rewrite my story.

As I made peace with being disliked, stuck to my truth, and persistently honored my boundaries and needs, life brought me the people who can hear, see, accept and honor me effortlessly. As I shared my experiences and healing tools through my events, courses, and blog, I started to witness how the women I touch also started to blossom. We need to understand that most of us have been operating from the victim mindset for so long while giving our power away and self-sacrificing for the potentiality. When we claim our power and start to operate from our truth, we might lose some dysfunctional connections on the way. Life creates space for better to enter. It's ok to end a marriage or relationship if it doesn't serve us. It's not failing; it is claiming what we deserve, what we want from life.

We all carry wounds around love. We learn what love is through unloving experiences. The love and care we couldn't get in our childhood is our light to bring into this world as adults. If you were born into a codependency pattern, it just means you have the strength to end it and become the cycle breaker. Know that the moment you decide to give yourself a better life and better relationships, life is ready to take you higher. After all, life is merely a reflection of how we love and treat ourselves. When we learn how to love and cherish ourselves with all that we are, trust me, life loves us better.

With love.

ABOUT THE AUTHOR

EZGI DEVI

Ezgi Devi is the founder of Wise Wild Wombmen community that empowers women globally. A spiritual teacher who gets her clairvoyance directly from the Source to make a heart-centered change in this universe. Through mindfulness-based coaching, she offers holistic therapies and workshops to support individuals in creating sustainable ways of living that suit human nature; and consciously activating health, wealth, and harmony in life. She assists with helping her clients take full power and responsibility for their journeys by understanding the universe and the nature of human-machine. She connects the dots between science and spirituality by blending her teachings with ancient healing tools and spiritual treasures that she studied with masters from all over the world. She hopes to inspire an enhanced education system for youth and a new structure for a society based on authenticity. She is also a sound alchemist and wanderer who produces soulful music for healing purposes, facilitating ecstatic dance rituals, sound healing sessions, and women's circles throughout her travels on this beautiful Earth.

Websites:
    https://ezgidevi.com/
    http://www.wisewildwombmen.org/

Instagram:
    https://www.instagram.com/ezgidevi/
    https://www.instagram.com/wisewildwombmen/

Facebook:
    https://www.facebook.com/ezgidevi/
    https://www.facebook.com/consciouslifewithezgidevi

HAZEL CRESSWELL-KING

I DANCED WITH MY SOUL

"Anything is Possible"

I couldn't ignore it any longer; it became louder and louder, more defined, more clearer with every day; I had to say YES to dancing with my soul. I didn't know where it would take me or to what, but I had to follow.

Little did I know it would lead me on the most incredible journey of my life, to reclaiming my sovereignty, remembering who I am as a divine soul, a glorious being of light; powerful and wondrous, how we all are if we just look within ourselves, listen to that all-knowing voice that resides within us, trust in ourselves that we will be led to the life we are truly here to experience.

So what did my soul lead me to, where did it take me, who did I become once I had said YES, WHO am I today?

As I sit here, I am truly blessed with the knowledge and wisdom of who I am. I am a woman who faced her biggest fear, who stared death right in the face and found life.

I am a woman who has shown great strength and courage, who has bared her soul so bravely and vulnerably, cracked open her heart and discovered the love she has for herself, who faced the shadow parts of herself, who healed the core wounds of her existence to discover her magic and gain the confidence to share her art with the world.

I am the woman who no longer feels afraid to speak her truth or share her wisdom, who has re-written her story, collapsed her time-lines from abuse, embodied her sovereignty, and found her divine feminine, the woman who is living a life led by her soul.

But like so many of us, that's not who I was.

I remember asking myself so many times over the years, "why am I like this, why am I so fixated on death"? I even remember as a young child not wanting to go to sleep unless mum told me she would see me in the morning. It was the only way I could close my eyes and feel reassured I would wake up the next day.

Even after having my babies, I wouldn't let myself sleep, no matter how exhausted I was, no matter how traumatic the births had been, I was so scared to just let myself relax, to just go to sleep, "surely I will die".

My births felt like near-death experiences, especially my youngest, I hemorrhaged with both of them, but this one was the worst. I remember seeing my husband standing in the corner of the room holding our baby girl as the medical staff around me tried to save my life; I only had to close my eyes, and it seemed like I would have gone.

My work would revolve around death too. It started around 20 years ago when I heard the first calling of my soul; I gave up a career in the NHS to set up my first business as a Spiritual Teacher but soon found myself wanting to help those at the end of life.

Before I knew it, my soul led me to the funeral industry, working in all areas of the profession, including setting up my second business as a Funeral Celebrant, during which time I also founded a Bereavement Centre.

All of this would take me to sit alongside a wonderful therapist in the centre; she volunteered her well-being services to my team and me. I remember how l leapt at the chance to take up her offer of counseling because, by that point, I was so ready to tackle the overwhelming fear that had resided within me for all these years; the fear of Death.

Not one day would pass by where I was actually present at any given moment. I was consumed with the fear of death 24 hours a day, seven days a week, and it didn't matter where I was.

I could never be present around my loved ones; I was always fixated on when or how they would die, how would I die, how would they be if I wasn't here, how would I feel if they weren't here, and it seemed stronger around my parents. It wouldn't stop, it wouldn't leave me for one moment, and it controlled my life.

One afternoon whilst sitting in our session, I would find the answer to the question I had asked myself for so long. Why was I so consumed with the fear of death?

In one given moment, a moment of utter shock and realisation, my body and mind finally allowed me to remember. I had been sexually abused as a child by my parents' best friend, George; I was threatened to comply by being told that if I tried to tell anyone my parents would die, I would die.

There it was starring me right in the face, the answer that I had longed for, and it turned out to be my worst nightmare.

I went through all the emotions possible, felt all there was to feel about being a victim of abuse, realising I had taken on the responsibility of keeping my parents safe all these years, I had tried to protect them all my life, became my mum's mum instead of being her daughter. I was constantly in a freeze or flight state, playing out the same existence over and over again, the same behaviours and patterns; yet I could also see how at long last, my entire life made sense.

As crazy as it seems, the clouds seemed to pass, and all the pieces of the puzzle came together, yet as they did, I began to realise I didn't have a clue who I was, I had been so disconnected from my body, my heart, and my soul that my head had controlled my life. I had lived a life in death.

With the overwhelming fear of my parents dying still residing within me, I just couldn't bring myself to tell them, I couldn't destroy their world, all that they believed in; yet one day, without warning, my soul urged me to tell.

I remember sitting that day with mum and dad as they watched my girls happily playing; I was as distant as ever, not present, just consumed by my thoughts.

Before I knew it, the words were coming out of my mouth, my heart was racing, and my hands were sweaty. "Mum, I need to speak to you and dad; I'm going to take the girls home and come straight back," "but I'm out tonight," mum said. "Mum, I need you to be my mum today; I need you to listen and just be there for me no matter what."

I took my girls home and drove straight back round. Mum and Dad were sitting on their sofa under the window with the sun shining through like a ray of divine light. I sat down with my heart racing once more and again, without any control, words just came out "I need to tell you something, something that will seem impossible, but it is true with every cell in my being, it is true. George sexually abused me as a child, and to protect myself, my mind had shut it out, but every part of my body remembers."

I don't think I will ever forget the shock on their faces, that moment of deadly silence. I went over to them both in tears, knelt on the floor, and just asked my dad to hold me. Dad had never been able to deal with emotions very well, and I could sense the embrace was making him uncomfortable. "Hold me, dad, let me cry like your little girl," I said. He did; he held me until I no longer needed to be held.

I left the house to go to the centre where I would meet my therapist for a reiki healing. We hadn't been in the session long before I started to panic that dad was in his shed about to hang himself, "Let me call him," I shouted, "I need to know if he is ok."

Of course, he was ok; it was just the reality hitting me that I had done the one thing I had been told not to do as that small little girl, and now I had to face the consequences. In truth, it was my soul leading me to face the awful fear that had controlled my entire life; I had to just trust and continue to follow its calling.

As time passed by, mum, dad, and I began opening up to each other, and for the first time, we found ourselves in a supportive, open, and honest space, trying to come to terms with something so difficult for us all to comprehend. It seemed to bring us closer by the day and led to so many wonderful conversations with each other; I began to see them for who they really were.

Little by little, I pulled myself up from the depths of despair, moved away from being the victim of abuse, and began to carve a new life for myself, to feel happiness in my heart.

Once more, the calling of my soul beckoned, and a year on, I was selling my home and relocating to a farmhouse in the middle of nowhere. For the first time in my life, I moved a little further away from mum and dad.

The house was my dream home; I remember crying as I walked around it for the first time; I couldn't believe it was mine, little did I know it would become the ultimate of nightmares; the weekend I moved into my beautiful new home, my loving, protecting, strong and steadfast dad took his final breaths. It would be like the punishment I had been so afraid of, the one thing I had dreaded, the one thing that had consumed me each and every day.

I had told them I had done the one thing I was told not to do, and it happened, my darling dad was gone, and my world fell apart.

Dad's first anniversary came upon us, and a month later, I would share in a beautiful day with my mum; we walked and talked in the sunshine, and before I knew it, mum was telling me the one thing I had told her and dad back on that day ,"I feel sure I was abused when I was little".

And there it was, the ancestral wound that had held us all for so many years, the wound I would later come to know as the one I was brought here to heal for our future generations.

Only a matter of weeks would pass by, and without warning, as suddenly as my dear dad; my best friend, my whole world, my beautiful, gentle little mum, Nanny Pammy, would take her final breathes to be by the side of my darling dad.

I was alone, devastated, empty, riddled with guilt and blame for telling them the one thing I had saved them from the last 40 odd years; I had done the ultimate thing, I had stood up to my abuser, faced his threats, and then lost my wonderful parents.

Mum's anniversary would come upon us, and in the December of that same year, I would find myself feeling as lost as I did the day they both died. Not only had my world on the inside changed, but the world around me had too.

The new year arrived, and I heard that ever familiar call, but this time it was to take me to something I never thought possible. I found myself taking recap training in EFT, and as I did, I began to see how I had fallen back into victimhood; playing out the same old behaviours and patterns as before, I was consumed with anxiety, and it was sucking what little life I felt inside, right back out of me.

In the moment of realization, I knew I had to pull myself up; I had to listen to my soul and get myself back on track.

I would find myself signing up to an anger embrace workshop, filling in the details on auto-pilot; I hadn't got a clue why I was doing it; something was just calling me.

On the weekend of the event, we began to release our anger through bodywork, and I could hear that little voice inside saying, "I still don't know why I'm here". As I sat down, I began to feel an overwhelming amount of anger inside, and before I knew it, I was screaming.

I was later picked to undertake an anger release and forgiveness process where I found myself sitting in front of a chair as if I was talking to the man that had abused me. I remember thinking, "I've dealt with this; I don't have anything to say". How wrong was I!

To this day, I don't think I've ever experienced anything so powerful in all my life, so life-changing mentally, emotionally, and physically.

The process would take me to the depths of my trauma, and I just trusted all would be well, that I was doing this for my highest good.

I screamed every word of anger that I had held in my body for 45 years, every single moment of guilt, regret, hatred, every single emotion that I had experienced through the abuse. I said everything I wanted to say to George, no holding back, open and raw for all to see.

The women in the group held me in love and compassion as they bared witness to my vulnerability, which helped heal the wound of not being heard or believed.

I reached a point in the process that allowed me to forgive my abuser for every single thing he had done, for how he had affected my entire life, robbed me of so much, and as crazy as it seemed, it was possible. I could finally be free of him; he could no longer have a hold over me; I was no longer a victim; I was now a survivor.

That night, I knew I would be a new woman when I awoke; I slept so peacefully for the first time in what seemed ever. I had experienced a total rebirth and, over the coming days, would see the physical changes in my face; I could feel it within my body, I felt so much lighter, so much younger; it truly was incredible.

As the weeks went by, I continued to notice many changes within myself on all levels, a sense of peace and knowing suddenly came from nowhere; I found myself with another layer of abuse to deal with; two more abusers that my mind had chosen to protect me from, yet my body was now clearly sending me messages that it was time to heal once more.

It was as if the first layer of abuse was a trial run, so this time I just faced it head-on without hesitation. "Bring it on", I remembered saying to the anger coach as I approached her for a private session, "let's deal with this devil and put it to rest".

This time, the process seemed even more powerful than before, it was a completely different level of abuse, and I would experience a massive death and rebirth process to the point where I actually stopped breathing for a few moments and then took an almighty gasp as my higher self took over and healed my heart, soul, body, and mind…..

This time it would take me two weeks to physically overcome the process; it only demonstrated to me how incredible my light was, how through answering that call, I had risen from the ashes like a phoenix. Nothing was impossible, and I could achieve all that my soul desired, so much so that within a month, I would hear the loudest call of my soul ever, and before I knew it, I had made the biggest investment of my entire life; I had signed up to a 12-month programme that would align me to my soul and its true calling. I had invested £18,000 in me.

…….

Mum and Dad had worked all their lives to give me a good inheritance, and it would be this that would help me to become the woman I am today. It took me a long time to see that though I was so afraid to spend it, I soon realized that I didn't need to invest it in material things or property. I needed to invest it in me, and it would remain with me throughout the rest of my life; it would always be with me.

Through the programme, I began to see the life I wanted, and it certainly wasn't one of drama and sadness, pain, or hurt anymore but a new life full of love, joy, and happiness. Of a soul-led life and business, my heaven on earth, and it wasn't long before I began to see the incredible possibilities that lay ahead.

That investment was truly part of my soul's destiny. It led to the reclamation of my sovereignty, my soul, of understanding everything, my soul's entire journey, and the wonder of me.

So you see, I am blessed with knowledge, wisdom, and clarity. I have reclaimed my sovereignty, and I am here now to help you reclaim yours, to reclaim your soul and all that you are, to collapse abuse from your past and present timelines, to free your ancestors from their pain and suffering.

I am here, as you are, to lead the way forward for our future generations and raise our planet's consciousness as we move into the new earth. I am here to show you that you can live your heaven on earth no matter what you have suffered…..

"Anything is possible."

ABOUT THE AUTHOR

HAZEL CRESSWELL-KING

Hazel Cresswell-King is a Transformational Alchemist, Quantum Light Healer, Intuitive Soul Coach, Channel for Light Councils & Published Author.

Her work guides those who have lived the life of a survivor from abuse to reclaiming their soul and its purpose, empowering themselves to discover their true wonder & magic and to share their soul's art with the world as they co-create a new earth.

She is passionate about collapsing the ancestral, past, and present timelines of abuse for our present and future generations.

She wants to see a planet that allows people to live their divinity on earth and creates a higher consciousness of love and freedom for all.

She resides in Norfolk, England with her partner Sonny & her two daughters Bethany and Lily-May.

Facebook:

https://www.facebook.com/Hazel-Cresswell-King-Transformational-Alchemist-Quantum-Healer-866527763682013/

Website:

https://hazelcresswell-king.co.uk

Youtube:
https://youtube.com/channel/UC-x4kY07o_AUSIiNlhVVgvg
Reclamation of the Soul Podcast:
https://anchor.fm/hazel-cresswell-king

JESSA LIN ROSE

SPIRIT SPEAKS IN THREES

*I*magine for a moment; you are directly connected to the Source of all Life. You have the ability to create past any perceived limitations; you are a bridge between worlds; you have the magical ability to see fairies, speak to trees, to see the truth of all time and space existing all as one entity. You can clearly, without a doubt, see the intricate connection of all things.

HOW WOULD YOUR LIFE CHANGE? Would you express yourself more freely? Be more open to exploring the unknown? Would you move through the world differently?

* * *

NOW, imagine you came into this world with these wonderful gifts, but no one around you could understand them...Would your friends, your family, society call you crazy?

WOULD YOU UNKNOWINGLY AGREE?

. . .

WELL, that's what happened to me...

I LOOK BACK and see clearly why I chose such an intense upbringing. It was a necessary part of my Divine plan. I chose what was necessary for me to learn so that I could fully step into and embody the woman, priestess, shaman, healer, lover and woman I am.

THE UNIQUE PROGRAMMING we receive from our upbringing, family, friends, school, community, society, etc. is an important part of our soul's puzzle to uncover the truth and return to our True Selves. To remember our soul gifts and welcome ourselves back to wholeness, we must be willing to look at the very things that 'broke' us in the first place.

AS A YOUNGSTER, my learned/programmed experience led me to not trust my emotions, experience, subtle body senses, psychic/spiritual gifts or myself at all. Gaslighting, abuse, drama, addiction, abandonment, blame and shame were part of the norm for me. When I tried to express or share what I thought to be true, I was told, "you're too young to know what you saw" "you don't really know what happened" "you can't make that type of decision" -which left me questioning if I had any grasp on reality. Not only did I begin questioning my reality, but I also began shutting off my spiritual gifts completely as a way to protect myself. If I was being told that I couldn't see clearly what was happening right before my eyes - then how could I trust the gifts from Spirit that no one else could confirm with me?!

BY THE TIME I hit adolescence/young adulthood, it became clear in my behavior that I didn't trust myself, I didn't know myself, and somehow, I came to believe everyone else, especially those who had authority over me, I believed they knew better than me. Without even realizing what was happening, I had given my autonomy, sovereignty, and power away to people, experiences, and things outside of me. I began trusting other people more than myself; my coping mechanisms had become my belief system. So I do my best to keep quiet, do as I was told, not question authority, fall in line, be the perfect 'business woman' 'girlfriend' 'daughter' etc. I played the game, I followed the leader and behaved and acted in a way that made others like me or numb myself out so that I could feel 'normal'. I often felt I failed to live up to some false expectation of who I was 'supposed to be'.

SIMILAR EXPERIENCES CAN BE true for many of us; the systems of oppression and suppression have been running strong for generations. And while it may not be 'our fault', it is an opportunity for us to begin to see where we can choose to do differently. No matter our conditioning and programming, we can consciously begin to uncover the truth and reprogram our experience in a way that is more loving, compassionate, fully expressed, and authentic, should we choose. It's not always the easiest road to pick, but it is so worth it.

MY RE-AWAKENING to my inner truth, mission, purpose, and sacred dance with the Great Mystery and Spirit of life began around 26 and has continued to unfold beautifully ever since.

I FOUND myself all of the sudden sick all of the time, my body screaming out in pain, mentally, physically, emotionally, and spiritually every part of me was begging for me to come back home - to learn how to pay attention and come back to my Soul's inner knowing.

* * *

What do you know about the sacred #3?

In many ancient communities, the number three is considered the perfect number. It is the number of harmony, balance, wisdom, and understanding. It represents past, present, future - mind, body, spirit - birth, life, death - beginning, middle, end - it is the number of Divinity. For me, it's one of the many ways that the Great Mystery of Life communicates with me. Most of the major shifts in my life can be traced back to this sacred number. So much so that I have begun to call it: *The Feather, The Brick, and The Mack Truck* as a part of my soul learnings and guidance.

* * *

At 26, it hit me - I was super f*ckin unhappy. My job was soul-sucking; I drank or did drugs almost every night to distract myself from how miserable I felt. My body began to revolt, and I lost some of the most amazing people in my life.

I look back now and see the signs that Spirit was sending me, as lovingly as possible, that it was time for me to come home to the truth of my Being - my mission - my passion - my zest for life.

The Feather - the most subtle signs, often ignored and sometimes drowned out.

For me, this showed up as how unhappy I was in my work and social life. I felt unfulfilled, trapped, stuck, and like there was no way out. I had been bred for this job; I was meant to follow my father's footsteps. Literally, at that point, because of the abuse and trauma experienced as a child - I actually thought my life depended on doing what my dad told me.

So, I worked a job that sucked at my heartstrings until I could no longer stand it. When I wasn't at work, I chose to numb the pain by drowning it away. I drank to excess almost every night of the week. I made a side business out of hosting parties, late nights, and drug-filled ragers almost every weekend - to the point that I came home one night, exhausted, burnt out - not knowing a single person in my home that knew me by name. I was robbed, cheated on. I felt completely lost - unable at that point to do differently but knowing something had to change.

Spirit kept sending more for me to see - because I still wasn't quite ready...

THE BRICK - LOUD, pretty clear - you can maneuver or fake your way around if you're clever or disconnected enough.

This sign showed itself to me by three important and impactful people in my life passing away all within 6 months of each other. Two of these humans were some of the only people, up until that point, who met me where I was. Who loved me just as I was, who opened me up to the world of love to me in a way I hadn't experienced previously.

Kathy C. saved my life - her love, her support, and her ability to see me in my struggle stopped me from ending my life as a middle schooler. Without her and her family, I would not be the woman I am today. When she died - I told myself it was going to be ok - but in reality, I pushed everyone in her family away and didn't show up in a way that I am proud of. I wasn't ready to look at it. I told myself, "keep going" and ignored the grief I was feeling.

Then Drake died, my mom's boyfriend of 14 years. A heart attack only 6 days after proposing to her while they were doing the cross-word together, leaving my mother in tatters. She didn't leave the house for almost 2 years. I didn't know how best to support her, so I continued to let my grief build up.

Last was sweet Zoe. How could the world lose you? You were so young, so wild, happy, and free. You were one of my first adult friends that showed me non-judgement. The only person to believe me when everybody else was talking sh*t and making up rumors about me. She took me in when I had nowhere else to go. She was one of the purest, most embodied, loving souls I have ever known. Losing her ripped me open; I had no choice but to learn to feel again...

When the brick hits - you know it - something shifts. There is no possibility for you to be unchanged when Spirit sends a brick into your life. It might not make sense at first, but when you look back, you will realize without a doubt that it was exactly divine and aligned for your highest growth at that time.

At this point, I knew something had to give, but I didn't know what it was. Honestly, I didn't know where to start but I knew I had to. So slowly, I began to shift, I began to open just a little bit more to the signs and synchronicities that Spirit was showing me.

THE MACK TRUCK - you can't miss it - it strikes you when you least expect it. But deep within you, there's a part of you that knows it's about to happen; you brace, you prepare, and finally, you surrender to the impact of it.

For me, this happened at the same time as the Brick was making its way into my awareness...sometimes, our signs and lessons come all at once. As I was traversing all of the loss, my body began its revolt to show me just how disconnected I had truly become.

After months of being sick, in pain, not knowing what I would look like when I woke up in the morning, I began my journey of health and healing. It was painful, to say the least. What could have been an easy blood test turned into 4 months of diagnostic testing, being poked and prodded like a science experiment, being put on crazy dietary restrictions, which led to massively disordered eating and amplified my already f*cked up body image issues as well as having me feeling like I was going crazy because none of the doctors would listen to me? After all of this pain and discomfort, I was diagnosed with an auto-immune disease that would massively change the way I was living my daily life.

When the Mack Truck hits, Spirit is showing you there is no way out of where you find yourself. That the only way out is through- to learn to accept where you are and how you've gotten there to surrender yourself to the experience and learn from it. The Mack Truck can be one of the most intense parts of the re-birth and re-connection to Spirit process. It is not meant to cause harm, just the exact amount of discomfort necessary for your growth. By choosing to surrender to the discomfort, you will make it to the other side more alive, more connected, and more empowered than you ever have before.

SPIRIT SHOWS us what we need to see and is always speaking to us - whether we're paying attention or not. Three years ago, after years of connecting to Spirit and listening to the signs and synchronicities, I found myself questioning a major career move. I knew that teaching at yoga studios was no longer in alignment with my soul's truth, but it was no longer serving me and was actually holding me in place. I also knew that it was going to take some clarity and support before I could make the decision and say goodbye. So, I opened up an inquiry with Spirit to support me in making this life change.

One day, as I was enjoying a meal outside and questioning this aspect of my life, Spirit shared a gift with me - a beautiful white feather fell from the sky right in front of me. It was a sign that it was time for me to spread my wings, but I was quite ready; my ego needed more clarity. At this point, I had been teaching yoga for 8 years, and I had no idea what was next for me. Attaching meaning and belief to things can make it a bit more challenging to trust the more subtle signs and synchronicities we receive. This is absolutely normal as we integrate the whispers of Spirit into our lives in a deeper capacity.

Another week passed, and I felt in every part of my soul that it was time to let go, but I was having a hard time. Teaching yoga had become what I believed to be an integral part of my identity - who would I be without this aspect of me? How would I be successful? Meet new clients? The list of inquiries went on and on; I couldn't quite see the path ahead of me but the deep knowing of my inner Spirit kept nagging at me. As I was walking my pup, Cookie, pondering, questioning, and trying to figure out 'my next steps', I tripped over a brick and fell flat out on my face. Lovingly, though not as gently as the feather, Spirit let me know that it was time. Spirit let me know a bit more clearly that if I didn't make the choice to leave, I would be stunting my growth and creating unnecessary blocks in my life. Spirit had me literally trip over a brick and fall full out to show me what was happening - if that's not loud and clear - I don't know what is!

I knew at this point that teaching yoga had to go, but I had no idea when, how, or what would come in its place. I was having a hard time letting go…this is totally normal and a part of learning how to move through life with Spirit and your own Inner trust as guidance. I was driving home from teaching at the studio; I already knew deep down that it had to go, but I needed confirmation from Spirit one last time to be 100% sure. I asked out loud for a clear, direct sign that it was time, and as I was asking, I got rear-ended by a Mack Truck while sitting in dead stop traffic. When you need it, ask for it, Spirit will always give you the clearest and most direct answer.

Sometimes our lovely ego can be the one who holds us in place. The Ego LOVES comfort and often questions the unknown. So for me, learning the language of Spirit has been so helpful on my path of growth.

Spirit speaks in Threes. When you can begin to open yourself up to the language of signs, symbols, and synchronicities, you open yourself up to a support network that works flawlessly. And yes, sometimes what we need is for Spirit to speak really loud and clear if we question or have not picked up on the more subtle energies that have been presented to us. Through our inner dedication, learning, and willingness, we become more attuned to the subtle signs, synchronicities, and symbols that are here for our souls' growth. The more in tune we are with the subtleties of the Great Mystery, our connection to our own inner knowing, the more likely it is for us to feel the flow, ease, and abundance in our life experience and the less likely we will need Spirit to speak through us via the Mack Track.

Flash forward after years of refining, learning, and listening to the subtle language or Spirit, and I am confident, loving, connected, inspired, and powerfully embodied in my inner knowing, my soul's truth, and my mission and purpose in this lifetime. From the knowledge of the sacred three, I have learned how to move through the world with more embodied inner confidence, knowing that I can handle all challenges that come my way with ease and grace. Through practice, each of us can learn the sacred language of the Universe, Spirit, God, and how it speaks to us. Your signs and synchronicities will be different from mine, but the availability of this information remains the same, it is available for us all in our own unique way. You get to learn how Spirit speaks to you. I invite you to look back at your life and see if you see any patterns of Spirit speaking to you in Threes.

Trust me; the journey isn't always easy - it's confronting; I've lost friendships, relationships, dreams have seemed to "slip through my fingers," things that I once thought to be true are no longer true. Because the truth is there is one constant in life - CHANGE- and Spirit is always there to support us through it if we choose it. What I've learned along the way is we're always on the right path, no matter what. Spirit is always speaking to us, but it's up to us to listen.

Even the darkest, most intense situations are a part of our sacred learning here on Earth's plane. Everything is perfectly designed for us to learn how to ride the ups and downs of life. Remember, do your best to keep your heart, mind, and spirit open - allow yourself to choose to see, hear, and remember the signs being presented to you from Source daily. The truth is - you are already directly connected to Source. This knowledge is available, and inside every single one of us, all we have to do is choose to tap into it...

ABOUT THE AUTHOR

JESSA LIN ROSE

Jessa Lin is a Shamanic Healer and Guide to the Unseen Realms, who supports others in activating and connecting to their inner knowing - allowing them to remember they are their own best healer and guide. With her guidance and support, she invites others to return to their connection to Mother Earth, higher dimensions, as well as reawaken their spiritual gifts, and return home to the pure sword of their inner truth. Her mission is to empower individuals to reconnect with the Divinity within so they may honor their vision and purpose in life. She believes through the expression and connection of Self we can more lovingly move through the world. Through collaboration, community, and trust we can heal and amplify our relationship with each other and Mother Earth from a place of respect, unity, love, trust, reciprocity, and prosperity for all beings.

Instagram:
    https://www.instagram.com/theonlyjessalinrose/
Website:
    https://www.jessalinrose.com

JOSHUA ZOPPI

FINDING LIFE AMIDST DEATH

*T*he journey to discovering my sacred dance with Spirit has been one of profound lessons and a remembrance of the support we receive from Spirit daily. People talk about receiving a calling to do sacred work, but what does that look like? Well, this is where I begin my story.

The man that I am today is not the man I was ten years ago. I have had to be broken down, rebuilt, rewired, challenged, had to face ugly parts - all to be authentically me. We each have our own journeys, gifts, and guidance that require being honored. As I unlocked the door to Spirit and found my tempo, I have learned to dance to the magical otherworldly music and trust the support I have found in the spirit world.

The first time I encountered a loved one in Spirit was at the age of 4. I had been in my room playing with my toys when I witnessed someone walking into the room. This person had entered my room through the window and not the door. She proceeded to have a seat in front of me on one of the little plastic lawn chairs some kids of the '90s had. My mother happened to walk past my room and heard me talking to someone. She opened the door, asking, "Who are you talking to?" Unbeknownst to me, I proceeded to tell her the name of a family member who had passed not long before this current encounter. Upon uttering the name of the person, she ran down the hall to grab my father. The next thing I knew, they were both back in the room with me. My father asked me to tell him again who I was speaking to and where she was in the room. I restated the name and pointed to the chair right in front of me. He asked me to give her a hug. I walked over and hugged what I saw as a person, but to them it probably looked like thin air. My father then asked me to ask the spirit a question; a very poignant question to ask a spirit - "What is she doing here?". I responded, "She's working." I told the ancestor that I loved her, we exchanged a few more words, and then the ancestor made her exit the same way that she had entered the room - disappearing out the window into a beautiful bright light. By the next day, my family had figured out the work that ancestor had come back to do. The father of this ancestor, who had a very hard time with the passing of his child, had been in Newark, on his way for a haircut, when he had a massive heart attack that took his life. It's believed that my ancestor was preparing for her father's sudden return to the spirit realm.

The first physical death that I had witnessed was around the age of 5 years old. My grandmother, who had breast cancer, was terminal. While I was able to spend some time with this grandmother, it was unfortunately her time to cross over, and I wish I knew more about her and her journey. I stood at the foot of the hospital bed, watched her labored breathing and the death pallor begin to set in. I watched as my mother and aunt took their positions next to her. They lovingly mopped her brow, told her that they loved her, and my mom reassured her that it was ok to go and that they would be ok. Just as soon as the transition from this side to the next began, it was complete. The grandmother I knew and loved was no longer with us. This experience left me not only with a lot of unanswered questions but was also difficult for my 5-year-old mind to grasp and understand. My parents were wonderful in trying to explain their understanding of death, but it still did not answer my questions or soothe my Spirit.

Over the next few years of my childhood, I would lose very important people to me; people who shaped my childhood and who I hoped would last forever. Some of the passing's were quick and some were long slow downhill declines. These continued losses only further made the questions in my mind burn about what happens after this life. Where did they go? Do they see the other people who have passed before them? Does Heaven exist? Can they still hear me? All these questions with no sources to explain the truth of the process to the child in the room was extremely frustrating. One thing was for sure... I felt extremely lonely on an adventure to discover what this all meant and to stare at the ultimate journey we all face in the end in the eye.

My mediumship gift was still alive and well when I was around 11 years old, but I grew up in a very spirit active home as a youth. I had other experiences with spirit that startled me because it was very real and a little disturbing. I had no guidance as to how to handle these experiences, so I asked God to turn the gift off.

As time went on, I didn't know what to believe in. Does God exist? What is the purpose of this life? Little did I know that the answers I had been seeking for such a long time were about to arrive into my life as I made it into my early twenties.

The door to understanding my guidance and God appeared through a connection of a professor at William Paterson University that would change my life forever. My now wife, Denise Saracco-Zoppi, appeared in my life at a time when I was far from understanding myself and my path through it. Right before I began my journey with her, I had one more important death to face. My Grandfather, who I bonded with in his later years and a person who I will always be grateful for having part of my life, passed away just as I was wrapping up my junior year in college.

I am going to share the story of this amazing moment I was honored to partake in as it changed my view of death forever. My father, who was at work at the time, needed me to go to my grandfather's home to claim my grandfather's body from the authorities onsite. I spent the entire ride to his home talking out loud to him in the car. I thanked him for the time I was able to spend with him, the lessons he imparted, asked for forgiveness for what I felt were transgressions, and gave myself the closure I needed. Somehow, I knew he was listening. When I arrived on the scene, I thanked the officials who were there, and realized I first had to step in to calm down a CHHA who was there as a fill-in to take care of my grandfather. She had never witnessed someone die before. Once I settled her a bit, I tried to steal a private moment with the body of my grandfather who was alive only hours before. My eyes beheld this amazing man in his bed at home. This was a man who had a full 94 years of life brimming with happy and tragic memories, was a hard worker, inventive, his laughter, a beautiful singing voice, lover of poetry, fan of baseball and horse racing - now lying before me lifeless. It was a lot to take in all at once but I began to just be there with him in the moment and that is when a new view appeared.

I noticed something different this time that my 5-year-old mind did not see way back when, and that was the reality that the soul animates the body. Everything that made my grandfather who I knew him to be in life was gone. His newly-shed physical body did not even look like him, and his body took on the appearance of a waxy mannequin. While I could definitely feel the void of his physical essence, my extrasensory perceptivity could still feel his Spirit standing in the room next to his body. I could sense my grandfather's spirit knowing that, soon, the family would gather to see him lying in state in his home. This set the stage for a transformative process that I had been praying for.

I INQUIRED, prior to my grandfather's passing, about studying with Denise, and was accepted by Spirit into the program. The passing of my Grandfather became part of my initiation into the next leg of the journey of a lifetime to change my stars and to begin my sacred walk. Spiritual growth, authentically being you, changing the programming, facing the pain, and conquering the fears became an everyday experience for the next 5 years to honor the path that I now promised to walk. I gave reverence everyday to the new friendships I was creating with my guides and the blessings of watching the work change my life. At some point through this journey with her, I had an opportunity to revisit death in a new light...this time to make friends and understand a different perspective on what death is and what it is not. The gifts I shut off at 11 began to re-awaken. I was starting to engage the spirit world in a new and fantastic way that was leading me to understand a larger perspective of how all of life is intermingled and connected. It brought reassurance that those I loved who passed before me were still there standing right next to me. What relief it was to know that my ancestors are there helping those of the bloodline still in the flesh. That old feeling of loneliness began to dissipate from my life for the first time. I decided to continue to grow and to never shut my gifts off again as they had a purpose, but I needed to discover how they wished to be shared.

The first step in all of this was to heal and re-write the fear programming to better understand the truth of speaking with the deceased. I learned to listen to the story that the departed needed to share and to understand what was keeping them Earth-bound. As the work deepened, I began to exercise the gift more; often working to understand what was being shared with me. I had to learn that this was a loving and beautifully sacred act to be the bridge for Spirit to communicate to those needing healing from the loss of a loved one. What an amazing opportunity to clue people in to the magic that everything they are looking for from those who have crossed is right in front of them. This included apologies from ancestors which initiated full-on inter-generational healing processes of my clients. The beauty of being able to do this work was unfolding before my eyes, and a glimpse into life's continuance after the transition from physical back to Spirit, has a deeper reverence and sanctity that I did not know before allowing Spirit to take the lead in this dance.

The steps to the dance are now becoming more complex, with new levels and layers added to what I thought was a simple routine. I never thought that the work would have me investigate the topic of death and soul midwifery. I took heart to the subject in my late 20s, wondering what it had to share with me. I found the other large piece of my childhood puzzle written on the pages of soul midwifery right in front of my eyes! I realized that this whole time I had been doing the work that was described since I was a child, but I had no name for it. I realized that this was another opportunity to assist a soul in the most beautiful transition it will ever make - besides birth - is the transition out of the body. In my work as a soul midwife, I have observed the beauty that begins to occur as a spirit begins to head home; the change in the physical appearance while the Spirit of the person drifts in and out. The gathering ancestors who are awaiting the final disconnect from the physical to celebrate their reunion in spirit. The beautiful procession that occurs as the ancestors take the hand of the loved one, who has just re-joined them, and guides them into the light.

This dance that I now get to partake in every day has shifted my entire life forever. I have seen more than 50+ people pass away. They were grandparents, great grandparents, teachers, friends of family, great aunts and uncles, neighbors, landlords, cousins, and the list goes on. I have seen everything from drug overdose victims to natural old age circumstances. I was a kid who grew up knowing death but what I failed to see was what death was teaching me about life. Beautiful awarenesses shared by the deceased taught me about living life on purpose, without regret, and that we get to create the life we want in every moment. We are the extensions of the lineages that we were born into, and we pave the way with our own legacies for the generations that come after. In each moment we are being surrounded by our loved ones and being reminded that we are not alone. Your ancestors are your biggest fans as you are making your own way through your life, blazing a trail, and leaving your mark. They are the first ones you said goodbye to before incarnating into the bloodline you choose and they will be the first ones to celebrate your return when you have finished your journey. The baton passes to the future generations whose decisions shape our collective futures.

I take a moment here to thank all the souls who have shared space with me over the years and the guides who have helped to convey the much needed messages of love, comfort, and closure to those still alive. I am grateful everyday to share my journey and will continue to show up to the work with a humble heart and a deep sense of gratitude for the interconnected knowingness that Spirit continues to provide.

ABOUT THE AUTHOR
JOSHUA ZOPPI

Joshua Zoppi is Co-Owner of Ayni Healing Arts Center, Psychic Medium ("The Family Medium"), Author, Soul Midwife, Intuitive Oracle, and Mentor.

Joshua's journey with Spirit began at a very young age. His psychic medium gift appeared at the age of 4 and has been fascinated with what happens to the soul since. In 2012, Joshua began to embrace the mysteries of the soul inside his Shamanic path. Death as a teacher has taught Joshua the sacredness of life and how to live with no regrets.

Joshua began his sacred work with Spirit in 2016. Since then, he has offered readings, supported those transitioning into spirit and their families, and facilitated hundreds of Shamanic healing ceremonies. In 2021, he expanded Ayni with a full wellness retail section in Newton NJ. He and his soulmate, Denise, mentor their students through the Ayni Sacred Mysteries School.

Website:
https://Aynihealingartscenter.com
Facebook:
https://www.facebook.com/aynihealingartscenter
Instagram:
https://www.instagram.com/aynihealingartscenter
Email:
aynihealingartscenter@gmail.com
Phone:
862-268-3213

KARRIE MITTEN

SUCCESS IS A FOUR LETTER WORD

"*Y*ou will NEVER be successful!" ...that's what I heard... that's what I listened to every day in my head...it was on repeat. Every time I was close to success, my limiting belief would tell me, NO...you are not worthy of success, remember? I would create some type of self-sabotage act to block the success!

You see, when I was a young girl, preparing to go to college, dreaming of what my life could be, I had BIG plans for my life! I dreamt of being an artist and making an impact in the world. I have a passion for people, and I love to empower people. But what happened that one night, I lost my direction.

We were having family dinner that night; I was about 17. We were talking about where I wanted to go to school, what I wanted to study, and what I wanted to do "when I grow up" (I hated that statement because I always felt like I was a grown-up in a child's body). My dad asked me, "Karrie, what is it you want to do after college? What will your study focus be in college?" I answered, with my heart beating fast as I was so excited about it, "Dad, I want to be an artist! I want to make an impact in the world! I'm not sure what that looks like yet, but I want to be a catalyst for empowering people!"

His response is what changed my life. Out of love and protection for me, he said, "Karrie, you won't make any money doing that", but what I heard him say was, "You will never be successful."

Soul crushing...but what I didn't realize at the time was how deep this hurt. I was a dreamer and had a dream to do great things. In that one sentence, the trajectory of my life changed.

I set out for college, moved away from my family, and decided to go to school and study graphic design anyway! Shortly after I entered the University of Illinois, I found out that I would need to apply for the art school after my freshman year. I heard the voice, "You will never be successful, Karrie, so why try? Why put in the effort?" My belief system was telling me I was not worthy of success. Soul crushing, again.

After a series of failed attempts to be accepted to art school (not surprising, as I seemed to create one self-sabotaging behavior after another), I decided that my dad would be happy if I studied Business Administration...so that was the default.

Around Christmas break of my sophomore year, my mom got sick, and when I went home for break, I decided that I wouldn't go back. I had no desire to finish my studies; I was not doing well anyways... another incidence of self-sabotage. I didn't finish college...why bother? I wasn't going to have success. Crushing my soul once again

Fast forward to living a life in a default pattern. I got married, went to work, working in a field that was sucking the life right out of me. I started out in customer service, and every time I moved up the ladder, I felt I became further away from living my dream.

From the world view, I had success. Even though I didn't have a college education, I advanced my career purely on motivation to prove the system wrong...that you don't need higher education to be educated, polished, and professional. I excelled in all areas of my life on pure resentment. I channeled my greed, my need for approval and turned my anger into adrenaline energy, outperforming all my colleagues. I was a success...on the outside. I played the part, looked the part, and dressed the part – sometimes at the expense of running up the balance on my credit cards. I talked the talk and walked the walk, but I was a fraud. I hated what I was...

And then comes baby! Don't misinterpret this; I always dreamed of getting married and having children. That was in my vision. And I married my soulmate for sure. But when I started having babies, I was a shell of a human. I was forcing myself to believe that I was happy. I mean, I had a good job, good income, my husband was on an upward spiral with his career (he just got his master's degree), we love each other deeply, and we lived in a house in suburbia! What more could a girl ask for, right? I had everything going for me...

Except I didn't feel it...I was living in a default pattern of my life. I was following the pattern I had set of making everyone around me happy. I followed the rules. I was a "good girl, good wife, good mother" ...so our family began. My son was born first, and I remember thinking, "My heart is full...now I can be happy" and I was happy as a mother! But, in reality, people, circumstances, and external sources don't make you happy (I know that now).

My daughter was born, and our family was completed. For the next 15 years, I poured into my family, blessed to be able to stay home and raise our children. I love my family with all my soul. But still, something was calling me...

I took community college classes (maybe now I should finish my degree?) ...I went to church and did Women's Bible Studies, I volunteered, I cooked, cleaned, and loved on my family. But not on me. If my family looked good...then I must be good, right? We went to church every Sunday, making sure that we all were perfectly presentable. I could certainly act as if everything was ok. Maybe I could even convince myself? I mean, if we look good, we are good...right?

Meanwhile, everything inside was crumbling...

When my children were in high school, I once again found myself struggling to find ME. I was constantly at their school, volunteering, running fundraisers, helping wherever...really trying to find my place. My identity was wrapped up in other people's opinions.

One day, when I was driving back to the school for the third time because it was football practice, and my son wanted a meatball sub sandwich, which I picked up and was taking it to him, I had a moment. I pulled over to the side of the road and began to cry. I asked myself, "Who are you?" I didn't recognize myself. I had become a shell of a human being. I thought I was pouring into my family by serving them when in reality, I was robbing myself of the joy of being me. I didn't even know who ME was!

So, I decided that going back to work would make me happy. I reentered the corporate world with the same chip on my shoulder…I was going to prove everyone wrong once again! I was under the belief that if I just worked hard, I would be a success, so I worked hard, harder than most, and played the part of a successful businesswoman that had it all together. Then that voice in my head would pop up and remind me that I would never really be a success; remember, Karrie? I was a mess.

I made every effort to convince myself that I was serving people through my job. I bounced around careers often because I was trying to find the one that fed my soul and answered my dream. Every time I changed my career, I fell further and further away from living my soul's purpose. I talked myself into thinking that selling digital advertising was serving people (I mean, look how much money you can save and how many people will see your product!). And, that selling information technology managed services was serving people (what if your system crashed?? You all would be out of a job, families would suffer!!).

Then, finally, I had an opportunity that crossed my path!

A friend of mine was looking for a partner in her staffing agency. She was preparing to retire in a few years and wanted to groom a successor. This would be at the cost of buying her out over a period of a few years – a substantial investment! My life savings and then some would be on the line.

I followed the money - the shiny, bouncy ball - and the advice and opinions of others. All my colleagues told me this was a great opportunity, that I would be great at this career, that I would make good money, and that I should do it….so I did. I convinced myself that this opportunity would serve my dream and my soul.

After six months of seeing the income potential – I had the money blinders on – I invested in the company, intending to invest (and borrow) more to buy her out. I paid no attention to my soul – it was crying and telling me not to do this, that this was not what I was being called to do.

I found myself, once again, depleted, empty, shallow, and miserable. I invested our life savings into this business, and it was literally making me sick. I had the old limiting belief screaming at me once again...YOU ARE A FAILURE! WHY ARE YOU CONTINUING TO DO THIS? YOU DON'T HAVE WHAT IT TAKES! YOU WILL NEVER BE SUCCESSFUL!

My life was failing all around me. My children were unhappy. My daughter started having anxiety attacks, my son spiraled into depression, my husband started having heart issues, and I didn't know how to deal with it all. My coping mechanism was to drink a bottle of wine every night, hoping all the bad stuff would go away. This behavior, this self-sabotage, just made it all worse.

One day at work, I had to deal with a situation where an associate that I put to work turned on me and told lies about me, my company, and her alleged injury. At this point, I hit rock bottom. I was devastated. I was rocked to my very core. I thought that putting people to work would satisfy my soul's purpose of serving people and making an impact...but I was wrong.

Now I was stuck; I mean really stuck! I invested our life savings in this company. My husband was fearful that we would lose the money if I left, so I felt I couldn't leave. I was in a place where everything around me was falling apart...but the worst part was that everything on the inside was falling apart too!

I felt truly stuck and didn't know what to do.

That's when I made a decision for my life. I drew a "line in the sand" and decided to truly go after what I had been dreaming about all my life. And let me tell you – fear gripped me! I felt fear rise up and clench me in the stomach! There was a part of me that said, "here you go again...not being successful! Why do you even try? What are you going to do now? What if you don't get your money back? What will everyone say? What if your husband leaves you over this?"

But another part of me was excited about my journey and looked past the fear. I let that part, the part of me that wanted my dream, win over the part of me that was afraid. I remember someone saying, "Great things happen outside of your comfort zone. Great things never happen when it's comfortable or convenient."

When I got back to my office, I decided that I was going to finally go after what my soul was calling for my whole life. I didn't know how or what, but I had been doing this "lone ranger" style for far too long! So, I sought out a life coach. I had been through therapy, and it did help temporarily, but I really didn't want to dig into my past and uncover the archeology of my life. I wanted to build up new architecture for my life - lay a new foundation.

After extensive research, I came across a program that spoke to me; that understood where I was and what I wanted more than anything; that fed my dream and my soul. This program taught me to dream again...like when I was younger and had big dreams to make an impact in the world. The staff made me feel as if I had far greater power than the conditions or circumstances of my life. This I knew, as this power had been calling me all along. I wrote out my vision and lived into it every day...putting on this life, feeling it in my soul, befriending it, falling in love with it.

In a few short months, I realized that this was my soul's calling! To do for others what this program did for me; it gave me my life. It reminded me of who I REALLY am and what I am REALLY here to do. I learned I am more than this body; I am a spiritual being having a human experience, and I am co-creating this life. Life itself is seeking expression through me, not to me, and is seeking expansion...what I have felt my whole life – WOW!

I loved the program so much that I decided to invest in becoming a life coach myself. I studied every day, drinking in the tools and principles, applying them to my life, learning how to teach them to others. I found my soul's calling!

I spent months preparing for my new soul's purpose and learned so much about myself and how this thing called life works. I learned that when our soul calls, we get to listen.

After my certification, I recognized that I couldn't be the only woman feeling like I did – pouring from an empty cup. My life's purpose became connecting with women who felt as if they were in a foxhole...doing life alone... "lone ranger" style...thinking that if they just keep putting one foot in front of the other, it would all work out. I now work with women who are at this crossroads...they feel life calling to them...whispering, "there's something more for you."

One thing I have learned is that life is not happening to us. This beautiful thing called life is happening through us and with us. Our life is made up of small moments strung together, and we get to choose every single day how to show up. We don't get to not create a life, and if we are creating a life anyway, why not create something beautiful. Create a life by design, not default. Most people spend more time planning a vacation than they do planning a life...but we are called in to so much more.

I love this quote:

"It's as if a king has sent you to a far and distant land, with one thing to accomplish. You could accomplish 100 things or 1000 things, but if you don't accomplish the one thing for which you were sent, it's as if you've accomplished nothing." – Rumi

We are sent here to earth, through human birth, to become the conscious being we are called to be, to continue to raise our level of awareness and follow our soul's calling. This is how we truly have an impact in the world. By raising the consciousness of our own self, we raise the consciousness of others.

My life now is rich...rich in love, rich in relationships, rich in health, rich in finances, rich in growth, rich in passion, rich in purpose. I don't look back with regret for the life I lived, but with grace, knowing that I had to grow through all that searching to arrive where I am today.

My prayer for you is that you listen to the whispers of your life calling you and take action on that calling. It is who you truly are – your true authentic, beautiful, spiritual self.

ABOUT THE AUTHOR
KARRIE MITTEN

Karrie Mitten is the founder and owner of Up Level Your Life Consulting LLC. As a certified, transformational Life Mastery Consultant, speaker, and coach, she has worked to find new ways of empowering women to live a life they absolutely love. Karrie became a passionate, heart-centered support system for women struggling to feel confident about their soul's purpose, and stuck in default patterns of life, typically by searching for the opinion and approval of others. She empowers women to tap in to their hidden genius and infinite power, and unleash the true soul's calling. Karrie locks arms with her clients and guides them through several programs, each tailored to empower them to live a life of design and she guides them with love, compassion, and experience, to live a life they truly love living!

Karrie has been featured in many podcasts and online events including "The Entrepreneur New Normal: Accelerating Beyond the

Pandemic", "Ready, Set, Pause" Podcast, " , "Wealthy Life" Podcast, the Mighty Networks "Soberful Life" Program, and has been featured in the Central Valley 209 Magazine. She also appeared on the TV show "The Apprentice"!

Website:
    www.uplevelyourlifeconsulting.com

KATY MARIE

ALTAR OF THE MOUNTAIN

I had finally hit my limit. I couldn't deny that strong and uneasy feeling inside myself any longer, the knowledge that I had to make some big life changes. I wasn't on my life path. Leaving my current life circumstances felt scary, yet staying felt more wrong.

This is my story of how I stopped living my life for everyone else and started listening to my inner voice and trusting my internal guidance. How I chose to jump into the unknown even though most people thought that I was crazy. For the first time in my life, I chose myself.

My life began in a little town within the state of Utah that is nestled into a beautiful mountain range. I grew up in a very religious Mormon family. As a little girl, I was taught a very specific path to follow in life to find happiness. My family lived our religion in every aspect of our life. We went to church every Sunday, served the other people in our community, prayed together, read the scriptures; my parents attended the nearby temple regularly. I was taught that I needed to abstain from all drugs, alcohol, and coffee. Being chaste and not having any sexual relations outside of marriage was burned into my brain all my childhood. You have to pay ten percent of all your income to the church. Women are to dress modestly and stay pure for marriage. Boys are to serve a mission for the church at the age of eighteen for two years. If you don't follow these rules, you can't go to the temple. The temple is the end goal of a Mormon. They believe that you make covenants with God in the temple that will help you get back into heaven. Without these, they won't let you in. They perform different saving ordinances here, including getting married. From the age of three, I was taught I must get married in the temple if I wanted to live with my family forever. This was my world.

I followed this path rigidly. I believed that if I didn't follow the strict rules, not only would I not be with my family when I died, but I would be shunned from the very dominant Mormon community I was a part of. I was very focused on fitting in. So much energy went into making sure everything was looking good from the outside. I believed that the Mormon church was true and put all my effort into living it. I was so worried about how others perceived me, and I needed outside validation to tell me that I was enough. Truth be told, I never felt good enough; all my efforts to be "good" were coming up short because there was a never-ending pressure to be more. More scripture study, prayer, temple attendance, service, more purity in thought and action, and guilt was my constant companion because of it.

The Mormon church taught me that the main objective for a woman in life is to marry and have children. I learned this as a young girl in my primary lessons and the songs we sang. I was married three days after I turned twenty. I had dated my then-husband for three months before we got engaged. We were so young and happy to be following the plan laid out to us. He was a good man and fully lived the Mormon religion as well. We started our life together. We were thrilled when we were able to get pregnant and start bringing children into the world. We were able to have four children together. The church highly emphasizes the importance of multiplying and replenishing the earth with children. Here I was on that path they told me to follow. I had all the things I was supposed to have to be happy, the husband, the house, the kids. I loved my children fiercely, and they brought me great joy, yet something felt so off inside me. I had done everything the right way, so why did it feel like I was carrying weight, a sadness? I was coming onto fourteen years of my marriage, and I had been struggling with this feeling for a while, but I pushed it down because my life looked like it was supposed to look. Yet deep inside, I felt so disconnected from myself. I was even starting to notice I was getting sick and tired a lot. To the point that they thought I might have MS. My body was communicating with me that something was wrong. After many doctor's appointments with no direct answers, I learned that it was severe anxiety but still didn't connect it to the fact that it was because I was suppressing my inner knowing and listening to others on how to live my life. At this point, the life I was living was still the only way I believed was the right way to live. Anything outside it was not an option in my mind.

And then my little girl arrived in our family. Looking into her innocent eyes so full of life started to stir something deep within me. Did I want her to grow up feeling the same way I did? The feeling inside me was getting stronger that something was wrong. I could no longer hide from it. How did I tell my husband about the internal struggles and disconnection to our relationship that I felt? How do you hurt a man you love, a good father and companion, by telling him that you felt the marriage was wrong and that you rushed into it too quickly? That even though there was good in your life together, that you knew deep down, it was time to walk away. If I walked away, where did I go? How did I leave my children and the only world I knew? There was a moment this knowing came over my body. It said, "Katy, you know what you are supposed to do, and you've known for a long time." This gave me the courage to finally voice to my husband at the time and family and close friends what was going on inside me.

As adrenaline rushed through my body, I expressed the pain that I had been carrying for so many years. As I voiced my truth, the people closest to me told me that I was crazy and would ruin everything. They said that I needed to keep pushing those feelings aside because I was married to a good man. I was crushed trying to ask for help and seeing that others were unable to give me any support. I see now that it was such a big life change, and their love for me made them fearful, and they were doing the best they could to navigate it just like I was. At that time, though, I felt as if I was drowning in the water and begging them for help while they were in the lifeboat, and all they said was, "you're fine, just keep swimming." Yet I knew I couldn't keep swimming. My heart was screaming at me that I wasn't ok. In that very scary moment, I knew I had to trust myself over everyone else. I had to start listening to myself. Even if I lost everyone and everything in the process, I couldn't keep abandoning myself. I couldn't deny the fact that I knew I needed to walk away from my marriage. I was scared to hurt my four children by breaking up our family, they were my everything, but this internal voice was so strong that I moved forward anyway. Once I listened and took a step away from my marriage, I started to see things inside the religion I grew up in that didn't feel true to me anymore. To realize that the religion I had devoted my everything to in my life was a lie was soul-crushing. This was so scary because my whole foundation of life was based on the things I was taught in the Mormon religion, which was gone now.

I had leaped. Jumping into the unknown and started to free-fall. I was scared; I had little support, I was starting from ground zero as I had spent fourteen years married and putting all my time and energy into raising children while my husband worked. I had no resume; I had never paid my own bills. The implosion of life as I knew it felt suffocating. I found a job and took care of the kids when I had them but deep within, I was barely surviving. Most people didn't under-stand me. Rumors were circulating about me around the community I lived in that I didn't want to be a mom anymore, that I'd lost my mind. I clung to the few friends and family who hadn't shunned me and kept pushing through the dark. Losing my faith in the religion I grew up in felt like I had been punched in my gut. Not being with my children all the time felt like a part of my body had been ripped off. Having to figure out how to financially provide for myself and my children would cause me to wake up every morning with a deep panic. Sleep became something I feared to do. I felt alone and deeply misunder-stood. It hurt; it all hurt. I had no anchor to hold onto, just me standing in the debris of my world that had just been demolished. I kept going even with this excruciating pain. I kept going even though every way I identified as a human was gone.

This caused me to go deep into myself to find a strength I didn't know existed. Who was I? Why was I here? What was my purpose outside of everything I had been told? I was discovering my spirituality without the rigid religion caging me in. It was a journey of trial and error as I navigated this unknown territory.

I had always loved the mountains because my dad took me into them from the day I was born, but I turned to them like I never had before. They called to me with a power that is hard to put into words. I started climbing peak after peak. I couldn't stop; I just had to keep pushing my body hard on the steep and unrelenting slopes. I realized that climbing them was my medicine. The mountain was teaching and healing me. The mountain being a powerful metaphor for what I was going through. I had this huge mountain to climb in front of me, so I went out and took on the mountains that had towered over me my whole life. Pushing myself beyond my perceived physical limitations every time. As I ran up them, my legs would cry out in agony and beg me to stop, but I couldn't stop; I needed more. I needed to feel the sturdy mountain under my feet. To sweat out the injustices I had experienced and the anger that raced through my veins because of all my emotional suppression. The mountain, she taught me over and over that I am strong. That I could rise above it all. That she would always stand underneath me as I rose. And when I would get to the top of her and look down, a new perspective was showered over me, and I felt deep joy and satisfaction. I felt my power and truth like I'd never experienced before. The mountains supported me and gave me the confidence to stop running from my pain. They taught me that pain is not the enemy but a beautiful teacher. They taught me that I was so much stronger than I realized, and I needed to keep climbing in life on this new path.

The momentum that I had created with my initial jump was set in motion, and with it came a magical shift. You see, I had finally listened to my inner knowing, and it continued to guide me. It was leading me down my path. It was taking me in a direction I didn't know but fully needed. As I started going inward to release old programming and find my true essence, my inner voice got stronger. People, places, and opportunities kept coming into my life that were so serendipitous that I knew it was more than just coincidence.

As I came back to my truth and started to see how amazing I was, starting to get to know and love myself, I knew I wanted to help others do the same because every one of us has an inner compass that will never lead us astray if we will listen to it. No one outside of you can tell you what is right for you. We have a system built into our bodies that is trying to speak to us, but we are so disconnected from our true essence and guidance within our heart and gut; so we rely solely on the brain and all the things we've been told to do with our lives. Yet the intellect alone is insufficient because it is full of false programming, and that's all we use to make decisions. When we connect back into our heart and gut, knowing we will be guided on our perfect path in life so we can live full of presence, passion, and joy, we can start to live alive! My body had been speaking to me when I thought I had MS, and it clicked within me that this is how I wanted to help others, to help them connect back into the wisdom of their bodies that are trying to communicate with them that something is wrong.

I wasn't sure if I should go back to school and become a licensed therapist or become a life coach. The second option felt scary because it was less conventional. Yet again, I felt the pull to do it, and I also listened to my inner voice to attend it in-person rather than doing it all online. That week of the in-person training changed my life in such a positive way from all the connections and healing that happened. Learning all about the subconscious mind and tools to help make real change. I met women who became my friends and mentors, which led me to learn about and become a breathwork facilitator. At the time my friend told me she was taking the training, I had never tried it but knew instantly, in my gut, I was supposed to do the training with her. It was so powerful and completely changed the course of my career. Here was a tool that helped me learn how to connect to my body in a whole new way. I started bringing breathwork into group classes, and the healing power in these experiences is growing like wildfire. People want and need this. I then learned about Gabor Mate and his amazing work in trauma. I was so moved by his documentary the Wisdom of Trauma but had no clue he had a course that taught people all over the world how to heal through a course called *Compassionate Inquiry*. I found out about this a month before the next year-long class started and knew I was supposed to join. I was accepted, and once again, this new information is changing everything on how I show up in my work and personal life. I now have the knowledge and tools to help people move the energy from their bodies that keep them from connecting and trusting their inner guidance system. As I hold a loving, compassionate presence for people, they can dive deep into the wisdom of their bodies with their breath to heal and come back to their true essence.

I have a very loving co-parent relationship with my ex-husband and his new wife. We choose to lead with kindness and work to show our children all the support we can. We celebrate birthdays together and have stayed a team for our kids as we parent. We have a solid foundation for our children to live on. I've also rekindled my relationships with my family. There is a deeper connection between us. Love was always there, and it can shine brighter now with our vulnerable authenticity. Healing myself has helped to heal all the relationships around me.

Listening to myself and taking that very scary leap into the unknown was the most important decision I've ever made. It put me on my life path, learning to connect to and trust myself. I'm aligning and waking up to my gifts and making my career out of them. It brought me to my purpose, which includes being an example for women and girls who feel oppressed. I'm living a life that feels fully supported by the universe. My passion is to help others see that they will never be led astray when they follow their soul's pull. They will be supported and held, and people, places, and things they never knew could happen before will come into their lives. I went from listening to others and playing small/safe to trusting myself and living big/free.

If you are reading this and feel suppressed and trapped, know that there is hope for you to live a life that is truly yours, one that is filled with deep joy and satisfaction. You can live a life aligned to your truth. The world needs us all to live from this space so we can leave our gifts and impacts on humanity. It's each of our birthrights to live life ALIVE!

Looking back, I've come so far, and I'm not done yet. I will continue to push, trust, and grow. I will rise up to my fullest potential like the majestic mountains have so lovingly taught me how to do.

ABOUT THE AUTHOR

KATY MARIE

Katy Marie is a Certified Breathwork Facilitator, Life Coach, NLP Practitioner, Hypnotherapist, and Compassionate Inquiry Student on the workings of trauma. Her work helps people heal the ways they have become disconnected from themselves so they can dive deep into the reservoir of wisdom that comes from within. She helps you live a life of passion, purpose, and vulnerable authenticity. Katy helps you to fully embody your truth as you shed the layers that are not yours so you can live life alive. She resides in Salt Lake City, Utah with her four amazing children.

Instagram:
https://www.instagram.com/hellokatymarie/

MICHELLE FOURNIER

MOVING FROM WHAT'S 'RIGHT' TO WHAT'S RIGHT FOR ME

This is my story of how I moved from doing what's 'right' to doing what's right for me. It's a story of Choice, Authority and Alignment. It wasn't easy, but it has certainly turned into a delicious dance!

There I was, 46 years old, standing at parade rest (a formal military posture), with my eyes focused straight ahead, getting yelled at by a man not much older than me. Both of us are high-ranking officers in the US Army. Outright anger spewing from him. Tears rolling down my cheeks, chin quivering, on the verge of sobbing.

There I stood, allowing myself to be yelled at and berated like a schoolgirl who missed curfew. And not a single word escaped my lips. How did it come down to this? How did I get here? Let's go back...

My Mom died of lung cancer when I was 10 years old. I was the oldest, with 3 younger brothers. My Mom was the fun one, always exploring life itself. My Dad was a retired Army officer and authoritarian. He was used to giving orders and having those orders obeyed. Our toy cars and rocking horses were always lined up; dress right dress! There were rules and protocols we were supposed to follow. Children are seen, not heard. However, the rules were never written down and could change at a moment's notice. Typically I didn't find out about a rule until I broke one.

I had my first calling to be a teacher when I was 9 years old. I was playing dress up, wearing my Mom's high heels, writing on a chalkboard and telling my imaginary class to 'Listen Up' and do what I say. Hmmm, wonder where I got that from? Hearing the click click of the high heels coming down the hallway was a symbol of authority to that little girl. I wanted that kind of authority. As I look back, I realize that I simply wanted to be heard.

When I was asked what I wanted to be, I proudly said, "I'm going to be a teacher when I grow up!". And then my Dad said, "NO! You're going to be a doctor, so when you grow up and get married and have kids and he leaves you, you can take care of them." Repeatedly, when I voiced my desires or opinions, I was corrected. So, I turned off my intuition at a very young age. Because, apparently, it was wrong.

I grew up quickly, now being responsible for helping care for my younger brothers. Everything was pretty serious. I will never pretend to understand the loss and total life interrupt that happened to my Dad. I did my best to not rock the boat. I learned at that young age to look outside of myself for direction and approval.

I did what was 'right'… but it wasn't right for me.

I strove for recognition. When I was in the Brownies and Girl Scouts, I did whatever I could to earn those badges. With a lot of badges, I could prove that I had value. Turns out one of the Girl Scout badges you can earn today is a Family Connection badge. I don't imagine our family would have qualified.

I joined the Army because of a cute guy named Kevin. He invited me to take an ROTC class, and I applied for and received a full-ride scholarship. I started out in pre-med (cause that's what my Dad told me to do), and it was hard! I switched to nursing and ended up spending 24 years as an Army Nurse. In the Army, I could earn badges there too! So I earned myself some badges by jumping out of perfectly good airplanes and rappelled out of Blackhawk helicopters. So that people could tell when I walked into a room what a badass I was. Not that I totally believed it.

Someone told me once that I'm the way I am because I joined the Army. I later figured out that I joined the Army because it was a good fit for me and the way I am. The Army was a place of direction and structure.

So I stayed. 24 years. I did what I thought I had to do to get recognition, approval, promotions, and 'security'. Overall, I had a successful career. I traveled the world; I had a community, I was recognized for my expertise and experience.

Until I didn't do what was right, or what was right for me. All because of a cute guy named Jonathan. (are you seeing a trend here?) He was enlisted; I was an officer. That was not condoned in the military – it's called fraternization. Oh yeah, and he was legally separated. Which means he was legally married. Hence, there I stood, getting yelled at and taking it. It never occurred to me that I had a choice to walk out or seek an advocate for myself. The truth is my intuition raised a flag when Jonathan and I first got involved. But I was used to not listening, full of doubt. And I so desperately wanted to be loved. And he was fun! Oh, how I loved the fun. My heart yearned for carefree! I forfeited my promotion to Colonel, my position as the Chief Nurse, and my military career.

Around the same time, I attended my first personal growth workshop. I learned about limiting beliefs, self-sabotage and how my thoughts will ultimately create my reality. I had a lot of self-doubts. On the outside, I portrayed that Bad Ass. Though I frequently sought out a friend to double check my decisions. I felt like a fraud – seemingly so put together on the outside and not so much at all on the inside. The most important 'aha' I got from this class was Possibility – the possibility that I could change, that my life could change, that there was hope. That I might actually be able to create a life I loved. And be true to myself!

And so began two decades of working on myself. I became highly involved with the personal growth company. I took the advanced courses and volunteered thousands of hours to support their trainings. The Teacher spark was reignited. I was doing presentations and damn good at it. I coached and co-facilitated some of their programs as a volunteer. I began pursuing the opportunity to become a paid trainer or facilitator for the company. There was no clear path or rule book. The carrot was dangled. I was given assignment after assignment to complete. I did everything I was asked and yet never seemed to quite qualify to get approval to be hired. In the process, I was being who I thought I had to be to get approval. I was doing what was 'right' but not right for me. For 15 years, I chased that carrot.

While I was figuring out what I wanted to truly be when I grew up, I spent another 10 years in corporate America. Climbing the corporate ladder in the civilian world this time. Starting out as a consultant and then a director in an international company. I wore dress suits and finally had on my high heels!! I was in front of the room 'teaching', giving presentations, and again, I was damn good at it. I was making a lot of money. But yet something was still missing.

By now, I was in a relationship with a cute guy named Lief. I was on the road 5 days a week, and that relationship became a weekend event. My time and efforts were going into my job. My relationship with myself was lacking. I wasn't fulfilled, and the thought of living this way for the rest of my life was depressing.

I was doing what was 'right' but it wasn't right for me. Our company was undergoing significant changes, and I was informed that my role was changing and given a description of my new responsibilities. I felt so constricted. I realized at that moment that I was living a life designed by someone else.

There are pivotal events in every life. I call them choice points. And there are pivotal people in every life; I call them soul friends – the people who will tell you the truth because they love you and want the highest good for you. I made the decision to resign on the day I was told what I would be doing in my corporate position. But wait, wasn't that what I wanted? To be told what to do?

My soul friend is cute too, and her name is Jessica. One day we were vacationing in Cabo San Lucas, and I said out loud – "I want to create a retreat for women called Piss Off Perfect". We had another Cadillac margarita, said 'cheers!' and didn't think much of it.

But I kept talking about Piss Off Perfect. Finally, one day, Jessica said, "stop talking about it – let's schedule it!" We did – and 6 weeks later, we had a full retreat. And all the women created tremendous transformation. They were amazed. And Jessica and I were even more amazed! Here was an incredible retreat that started with my idea – the currency of the Universe – and we did it! We didn't know how and we did it anyway! I was so proud! I did what was right for me! That was my first real acknowledgement of what it truly meant to be soul led, to follow my heart, and to celebrate my life by my design.

I began listening to my heart and following my intuition. I knew it was time to let go of the corporate world. I completed 2 coaching certification programs. I earned my certification as a Master Practitioner in Neuro-Linguistic Programming (NLP). And I began talking about starting my own business. I started dreaming about teaching again. I knew I had a gift and a message and wanted to share it. I had the burning desire to make a difference in the world, to help other women discover and claim their brilliance on their terms. But who was I to this? Besides, my only experience as an entrepreneur had been selling Girl Scout cookies all those years ago.

Once again, Jessica said, "Either go do it or stop talking about it!" Jumping into a new business at the young age of 61 was a lot scarier than jumping out of an airplane. It's probably safe to say that starting a new business at the age of 61 is not on the list of good choices for most people. It wasn't the 'right' thing to do, but it sure was right for me! I was finally following my heart, my intuition, and not what 'I was supposed to'. And boy, was this a pivotal choice point for me!

I chose me and decided for me. Without really understanding what I was doing. The (My) Knowing is what I stepped into. The Knowing is that connection to Source, the certainty of direction and calling. I have a thriving vocation with a powerful message. And honestly, I am in the happily ever after! It does exist! That cute guy, Lief, put a ring on it! We have a healthy, intimate, and fun relationship. That's right; I'm having fun! I love my life!!

Here are some of my learnings:

I've experienced an evolution of choice. As a 10-year-old I literally had no choice. It was my Dad's way or the highway – and since I didn't have a license, it was my Dad's way. As a 46-year-old woman being yelled at, I didn't realize I had a choice and that I could advocate for myself or seek someone who would. I can walk away from anything or anyone that is not in alignment or does not serve my highest good.

I now realize I always have a choice. I was so worried about doing it wrong. Though that was about others. I never considered the considerable damage I created in my life by making me wrong. I'm so grateful I no longer make me wrong! I choose me! And making a choice that is in alignment with me is always a winning choice.

My journey has really been about discovering that I am the authority in my life. I am the person who calls the shots for me. I truly can live a life by my design. And when I default to the design of others, it is still by my design. The authority I was looking for outside of me was in me all along. I also separated the authority of teaching (pay attention, listen to what I say) to delivering a message. The power is in self-discovery. The highest kind of teacher reflects to us our own wisdom. This is what I aspire to. I know my learnings; only you know your learnings.

I spent so many years looking for the 'right' answer. The right answer is the answer that is right for me at the moment. I've let go of other people's rules, especially when they are not clearly expressed. I had no chance of being successful on someone else's terms if I didn't know what they were. My true chance of success is being successful on my terms. When we follow 'what's right', we close ourselves off to 'even better still'. And the "even better still" is the allowing of the Unfolding of the Universe and all of its Infinite Possibilities. After all, how can we ever expect to have a perfect plan to get somewhere we have never gone before? The Universe has way more ideas, resources, and paths than we could ever imagine!

I've always loved to dance. Life is a dance. In my dark moments, dancing always raises my vibration. In my light moments, dancing is a celebration. Choose your music and your beat. Bust a move! Allow the unfolding of the Universe. When I'm in alignment, I'm in the flow and everything works. When I'm resisting, 'trying', chasing, or desperately seeking something outside of myself, that is force energy. Life doesn't work well through force. With flow comes peace. Flow attracts harmony and aligns resources. I now dance in my choices without explanation or apology. When we follow our hearts, or as I love to say, live a life that makes our heart sing, we create the delicious. And I chose the delicious!

I'm so grateful for the lessons of my past. My caution to you is to be informed by your past, not anchored to it. Take the positive learning and move forward. There's a saying that 'If you take a leap, the net will appear'. I'd like to suggest that if you make a choice for what makes your heart sing, the leap will appear. I took the leap! I'm now an award-winning international coach helping women create a life that makes their hearts sing. Jessica and I are still leading our sold-out Piss Off Perfect Retreats in Colorado and Cabo every year. I'm using my NLP expertise to help my clients eliminate self-sabotage, negative emotions and limiting beliefs. I share with them a proven system to create a life that makes their hearts sing. And I love the liberty I have in being able to coach anywhere in the world – especially near the beach and golf courses around the world.

One of my favorite lines from the movie 'A Few Good Men', at the end of the movie when the senior ranking Sergeant is answering the junior soldier's question "What did we do wrong" after they were convicted for doing what they were told to do. His response was: 'we were supposed to fight for people who can't fight for themselves.' The truth is each of us has the right to advocate for ourselves and what lights us up. And to show someone else the way. As it turns out, apparently, I don't need to wear a badge on my chest or arm to have honor and value.

This is the happy ending! And it doesn't have to end, does it? I've decided on the delicious. Won't you join me??

ABOUT THE AUTHOR
MICHELLE FOURNIER

Michelle Fournier is the ultimate Possibilitarian, Master Mindset, Life Coach, author, speaker, and comedian. Michelle uses her life experiences, including 24 years as an Army Nurse who jumped out of perfectly good airplanes, to give you the tools you need to free your authentic bad-ass and create a life that makes your heart sing!

Michelle works with women who are successful and yet feel unfulfilled; looking for a change but don't know what or how; still looking for their purpose, or are stuck in the rat race and don't have an end game.

An Intuitive and certified Master Practitioner of NLP, she uses a proven innovative system to break through self-sabotage and accelerate lasting transformational change.

Michelle's passion is to help you create a life where you are Free to Be You – without apology or explanation.

Michelle lives in Denver, Colorado with her person loves golf and white Oreo cookies.

Website:
 www.michelle-fournier.com
Personal Facebook:
https://www.facebook.com/michelle.fournier.359
Instagram:
https://www.instagram.com/thefournierformula/
FB Group (The Fournier Formula):
https://www.facebook.com/TheFournierFormula
Email:
michelle@michelle-fournier.com
Linkedin:
https://www.linkedin.com/in/michelle-fournier-a354288/
You Tube:
https://www.youtube.com/channel/UCYZUoXQihq4-kgAn3adyApQ

NICKY BURKE

DISCOVERY FROM WITHIN, MEET YOUR HIGHER SELF, AND RECLAIM THE POWERFUL MAGIC OF YOUR SOUL

*J*n the comfort of our own magic, we can gently focus on the forever unfolding puzzle of our lives with ease and grace. From the time I could walk, I was obsessed with jigsaw puzzles; my nanna would take me to the local Saturday market each week until finally the vendor turned to us both and said, "I don't have any more puzzles; she's done them all!!!" As a child, nothing made me happier than sitting alone or with my family as we gazed at the beautiful picture we were about to create together. My anticipation grew as we unsealed the box with great care, revealing hundreds of mixed up pieces, each one turned over with an excitement which I can only describe as the opening of an advent calendar door, surprising you with a sweet gift. We would arrange our pieces into piles such as castles, skies, mystical creatures, and swirly writing, a technique that I gladly adopted with my skittles and smarties, organising them into their colours and individual flavour for the pure joy it came with! I always wanted the orange and blues over boring brown as I knew I could make lipstick of them, surely I'm not the only person …. And well, isn't that what life is all about? Savouring the abundant exploration of life? At this young age, I loved my ability to focus, to create beauty, and then knock it all down like a big game of Jenga, so I could start all over again. As children, we are open and flexible, ready for new, so why do we grow fearful of letting go? Why do we fear that pieces of our life puzzle are missing or that we missed out on the instruction booklet that everyone else seems to have? Where does this doubt come from when we are born KNOWING our wholeness, knowing our wellbeing, knowing that we are the creators of our own experience and that life is about welcoming the adventures of the unknown …

I'm here to tell you that it is only through conditioning, experiences, trauma, and self-limiting beliefs that you will ever feel stuck in your life. You have simply forgotten your own magic. So, if in this moment, the idea of moving forward in life scares you, recognise that emotion is your inner compass, and the negative energy is letting you know that you have simply disconnected from your higher knowing. Just for a moment, I want to give you an invitation, to remember a time when you simply allowed yourself to be. Can you close your eyes and surrender to a moment when you remember the joy of playing? Or when you were captivated by the ecstasy of unconditional love? Or perhaps when you felt no responsibility to be or do anything? Can you remember your own innocence? Taking slow breaths in and out, I invite you to feel all the emotion that comes up for you; you are exactly where you are supposed to be in this moment. Grab a paper and pen and surrender for 5 minutes in your own gentle practice to feel the untouchable part of you that is forever whole. See you in 5 :)

Now that you remember, hopefully grinning cheek to cheek, I want to tell you that contrast is all part of the programme. Thoughts often come up for us, such as "Should I have done that differently?" And "Why don't I have it all NOW?" These are simply limiting beliefs … BLAH BLAH BLAH!

An exemplary version of our unique sense of being here can be found in the movie the "Labyrinth." In the movie, we are introduced to our hero, Sarah, who enters a strange world after her baby brother, Toby, has been stolen by the Goblin King; the only way she can get him back is to go through the Labyrinth and find the castle. She is quickly met by a tiny worm who hears Sarah's frustration "both directions look the same" Sarah wines, to which the worm advises her, "Don't go that way, never go that way!" Sarah takes the worm's advice and thanks her. When Sarah exits the shot, the worm speaks to the camera, "If she'd gone that way, she would have gone straight to that castle!" LOL!!!!!!!!!!!!!!!!!!!!!!!!!!!!!! The irony, beauty, and truth is that there would be no story, no growth, or inner triumph without Sarah's search, which leads her to meet her own divine power. (Along with new friends and magical creatures that try to take off her head off in the process - such a great movie, I highly recommend it!)

So ... when the walls come crashing down, and you feel that you're falling through a never-ending hole of darkness, where can you take a stand? Are we even supposed to? Or is life teaching to surrender? To surrender all control, illusions of constraints, co-dependency, and the need of being seen, heard, and loved in a particular way? What is your true calling for being here, and why, oh, WHYYYYYYY is there contrast, challenge, and drama? Why isn't it all free-flowing and cute like the beginning scenes of Bambi (we all know how that goes ...)? The same journey is taken by characters like Simba in the Lion King, Aerial from The Little Mermaid, and Thumbelina. Each hero begins in their innocence; they are called to face challenges and defeat their dragon, resulting in receiving their true wisdom and heart. My friends, you are made of the same magic; you were born to experience the contrast and expand into the divine truth of who you REALLY are! I honour you wherever you stand in your journey; you are so loved!

I had yet to begin any kind of spiritual practice; however, I had been writing in my journal for as long as I could remember. The ass-kicking truth of life after graduation was pretty hard to bear; I attracted fake casting calls, unpaid work, and manipulative directors; yes, the Me Too movement was happening on all levels of the indus-try. I needed a break! So I did what now seems so out there ... with ZERO training, I climbed the largest freestanding mountain in the world, Kilimanjaro. Why did I do it? I knew I needed to focus on something else; to find the true strength of me, I needed to get out of my victimhood and begin to trust my higher calling, so I did it. It was two weeks of visiting slums in Nairobi, dancing with orphanages, and experiencing the physical and mental hurdles that came with a 5-day hike up an all-terrain mountain. When we came down, and I sat in the van that would take us back to our luxurious hotel, tears streamed down my face. I was different. I felt that I had left a part of me on the mountain, the worry, and fear that I wouldn't make it home subsided, and I could only surrender to a rising truth within me. A lesson so beautifully put in one of my favourite musicals WICKED "You had the power all along, my dear." by GLINDA the GOOD. I am in no way suggesting that you follow the same path as I and physically climb a mountain, our climbs are as much internal as they are physical, but once I did something that was so out of my comfort zone, I realised anything was possible. More importantly, I found that my journey began 11 months earlier, from saying yes to the project to raising funds and choosing to know that I could make a difference in this world; I had finally come home to myself & realised that it was the journey of life that I wanted not the destination.

As I returned back to London, I felt my achievement gave me a new lease of life. I committed to more creative workshops that ignited my talents; however, reframing my emotional wellbeing from feeling powerless to powerful was not a journey I embodied overnight. Without boring you with the incredibly long list of illnesses and pains I created, here were my "wake up" moments

Just hours after exiting a relationship, my body showed me, "girl, you are OUT of alignment." My inner beliefs rose to the surface like wildfire! Whether guidance is received as a physical symptom, pain, or dis-ease, the body talks.

2) The "end of the career" injury. When everyone told me this couldn't be fixed, you'll just have to change career (basically give up on my dreams!) I just knew there was another way. It was the universal kick up the ass I needed to work with my intuitive nature, and I handed myself over for the very first time.

"OK, body, let's talk." I identified that over the 24 years of dancing I had never stopped and asked my body what she needed, I had simply pushed her to look, be and do what I wanted. I did love her, but this dysfunctional relationship where my mind was the master and body the slave was over. Slowly with tools, I'd been given and many of my own creations, I established a new relationship of love, trust, and freedom; I began to love myself for who I was for the first time in decades. A powerful meditation that helped me transform my feelings of self was where I found myself on a beach, looking over at dolphins and gently meeting people in my life; whether past or present, I actively choose to let go or alchemise the relationship. I would come out in rivers of relief; I had no idea what I had been carrying energetically. Each day, I grew stronger, wiser and as Abraham Hicks says, "I lay new pipes." My world instantly changed.

In less than six months, I was granted £5,000 from charities to help me financially whilst I healed. I created living in a new million pound home in London, amazing work opportunities as an artist and choreographer, but most importantly, I showed myself great love, a love that brought me new relationships. Previously I didn't have the ovaries to ask for money, but because I had lifted my vibration, shame changed to courage, courage to love, and the world seemed new again.

My soul felt freedom, not only when I danced but in LIFE!

In 2017, just days after my breakup/wake-up moment, I saw the advert "1 male and 1 female dancer to Jive in music video," accompanied by a small note, "they will also need to choreograph the video." I tuned into my higher self and called one of the best dancers I knew in London. "Hey, I know you don't Jive but give me one hour, and I can teach you." He agreed, and in an hour, we had our audition routine. As we stood in the corridor, we saw many couples who looked like Ballroom and Latin champions and clearly had been dancing together for years. We had only worked together on a couple of gigs, but our passion stood us out a storm! As we entered the room, we played the music, began dancing on the tables, and lifted the entire room! We were there because WE LOVED our craft, and within 30 minutes, I had an email saying, " we have to see more dancers this afternoon, but please, can we pencil you?" And the rest is history; we had an amazing shoot day, one of the best of my life because I didn't allow the old beliefs to keep me away from my heart. When I applied for the job, I didn't know the band was Scouting for Girls or that I'd gain my first credit with Sony Entertainment, and I really didn't know I'd receive loving comments from an audience of over 750 thousand people on Youtube, and still counting! I just knew that my heart called me to be free, to leave the past in the past because that is where it belonged.

My students were telling me of their new successes which they believed were a representation of smashing beliefs in my dance class and it was clear that my vibration had changed as I was being visited by ancestors & seeing non physical energy. I had no "woo woo" background, but something had opened up, and I fully plunged into my spiritual path. Over the years, I held ceremonies and initiated myself from girl to woman, from dancer to creative director, and from diary journaler to published writer; my prayers and asks were being answered daily by the universe, and I no longer leaned on dancing to feel good, I was LIVING the "Sacred Dance."

As an artist, I have lived a life creating from visions and my intentionality so I could receive jobs, opportunities, and the intuitive whisper of new levels of expansion. I realised that my whole world was changing because energy is everything. Remember those dragons I spoke about? Well … I was ready to face more of them because the inner knowing that the universe was giving me all I wanted was enough of a deep resonance for me to take this practice into more areas of my life.

It's Christmas 2020, and my intuition tells me to watch Home Alone. There is a scene when young Kevin is approached at church by his "scary" neighbour, who asks if he can sit next to him. Kevin freezes at first but realises that the old man is not scary at all; he simply carries a sadness. He shares that since arguing with his son years ago, he personally fears that his son won't talk to him if he calls to make up. Kevin assures him that he has nothing to lose, and in one of the final scenes of the movie, we see the old man clinging on tightly to his granddaughter and smiling at Kevin with tears of thankfulness. This is the journey that I chose to take with my father, which allowed me to release my own limiting beliefs that I was not good enough, heard, or loved in the world. With each step forward, I chose the possibility of days laughing in the sunshine together over the fear of rejection or any anger I may feel. I knew deep inside of me that it was the illusion of our differences that kept me from receiving my dad's love; in truth, he would tell everyone about my successes and how proud he was of me. As our bond deepened over the years, I could see the innocent child in his eyes mirrored by my own heart; the universe had heard my calling. Ego does a good job of trying to keep love out, creating separation, pain, shame, and the big one blame, but when we choose to connect to our higher self, we meet our true power, love! Before my father recently crossed over, our friendship blossomed to all I had wished for, and now we share a new kind of magic as he continues to let me know, "I'm with you." I feel blessed beyond measure! Not only because of the cosmic and comedic relationship we have but for the personal realisation through my own story that source/universe loves me completely as I am in every moment. I know that my inner being is always rooting for me, and with this knowledge, I stopped giving myself such a hard time; I stopped giving others such a hard time and realised that everything is simply attraction. RELIEF!

My story and your story are the same, one of strength, not sorrow. Growing up, my idol Cher saw me through high school with her strong diva lyrics that made me feel like the ultimate star she is, and we all are! The movie Burlesque holds a diamond of a song, "Haven't seen the last of me." The lyrics go "I've been brought down to my knees, and I've been pushed, right past the point of breaking but I can take it. I'll be back, back on my feet, this is far from over. You haven't seen the last of me." This song is the most divine example of the rise of the human spirit; from feeling broken to overcoming her own fears; she reminds HERSELF of who she TRULY is; this is available to all of us!

I've found so much sanctuary in the White Spring of Glastonbury over the years; on my last visit, I stepped in and asked for guidance to let go of anything that was no longer serving me. Within thirty seconds, I felt an overbearing love surround me, and I wept for what seemed like hours in the dark shadows of the sacred pools, lit by pilgrim's candles. I placed my right hand in the sacred waters and said thank you. I saw my nan's ring shining at me under the cool waters, sparkling like she, a woman who practically Cha-cha-chaed her way out of her physical life and into my heart forever. As the beloved ring glistened, I realised how much of a new woman I had become. Through writing and speaking with my inner being, I pulled myself out of the emotional and financial gutter and to a new place where I can now look in the mirror and finally say I love you. Through vulnerability and caring about the way we feel, we can embody the sacred dance of life with freedom, self permission, and expression. I truly believe that until you own your story, it owns YOU! So here's your chance, it's time to reclaim your power. With deep love and appreciation.

ABOUT THE AUTHOR

NICKY BURKE

Nicky Burke is a Professional Artist, Choreographer, Creative Director & Intuitive Coach.

Her clients include the BBC, SKY TV, ITV, Sony Music Entertainment, Channel 5 & ExCeL London, including Uber, Eats, Harry Hills Tea Time Series, Lip Sync Battle UK, Britains' Got Talent, Scouting for Girls & more. She also works on feature films & guides singer/songwriters worldwide.

Nicky's passion for dancing led her to share the joy of movement with people all over the world of all ages and abilities! Her teachings support shifting old belief systems and subconscious blockages so you can open up to live a life of your own unique gifts. Nicky brings her wisdom and compassion to every board meeting, set, and coaching session knowing that each person is on their journey. You can hire Nicky for private and group sessions, both online & in person, enquire today to reveal your SUPERPOWERS!

Personal Website:

www.nickyburke.com

IMDb profile:

http://www.imdb.me/NickyBurke

Nicky Burke Productions Youtube Channel:
https://youtube.com/channel/UCsfaMudUvP1qGYhC4Z9dPUw
Brainz Magazine Published Writer & Podcast:
https://www.brainzmagazine.com/executive-contributor/Nicky-Burke
Linked in Profile:
https://uk.linkedin.com/in/nicky-burke
Instagram:
https://www.instagram.com/burke_nicky
Nicky Burke Facebook Business Page :
https://www.facebook.com/NickyBurkeLDN/reviews
Inner Glow Dance Community Page:
https://www.facebook.com/groups/innerglowdance
Discovery Call Link:
https://calendly.com/nickyburke/your-personal-discovery-call

E. nicky@nickyburke.com,

SARAH NEWTON-SMITH

PRE-DESTINED OR DIVINE INTERVENTION?

The birth of my son birthed my soul into a completely new way of living; it dissolved my world-view as I knew it and kickstarted the awakening of a lifetime.

At 14.38 on the 11th of March 2015, he finally arrived. I couldn't believe that the weeks we had spent in hospital could finally come to an end. My son was here, and after an extremely traumatic and painfully indescribable birth, I was finally able to meet this tiny little warrior, a warrior who would later become a pivotal and monumental catalyst for my soul's growth.

Archie was born weighing 2.1 lbs; his tiny eyes stared up at me from his incubator; he was absolutely perfect. The son I had always dreamed of. Archie, the name that my daughter Abbie had chosen for him, was very fitting and at 28 I was ready to step into the role of being a mummy for a second time.

It wasn't long before I was able to bring Archie home and the magic that he created had started to unfold. You see, Archie was a crystal child; I knew nothing then about what a crystal child was back then; however, after gaining a greater understanding of what this meant, I realised how much of a blessing it truly is.

Crystal Children are all very special; you may even have a crystal child in your life. These highly intuitive and emotionally in tune children are easily labelled as having extra sensory perceptions or easily affected by loud noises, sights and sounds. They are sensitive to the emotions of others and can become easily overwhelmed in highly stimulating environments. Archie was no exception; I could feel that Archie had a soul level awareness and spiritual connection that ran deeply throughout his entire being. I later came to understand that Archie had come here with a specific soul mission; his first mission was to kickstart an awakening, a waterfall effect of my own soul's evolution.

When Archie was 4 months old, I began to notice that things around me had changed; more specifically, things inside of me had changed. I could feel that my intuition had started to deepen significantly. I recall the first time this happened to me, I could hear the phone ringing in the next room; I walked towards my phone sensing that it was my mother on the other end, I reached for it and to my bemusement it wasn't ringing, nor was there a missed call. I slid my phone into my pocket and within moments, I could feel the vibrations, my phone was ringing, I was silent for a moment before I answered "............ Hello, Mum?"

Over the course of the coming months, intuitive thoughts and beliefs kept flowing through to me at an increasing rate. I started to experience feelings that I could not define as mine. What was happening? Why was I now feeling things I had never felt before? Hearing things I had never heard before?

It was a strange concept to me, but I paid little attention to it. It wasn't long before the cracks in my relationship started to show, and Archie's father and I decided to separate; it had been a turbulent and sometimes volatile relationship so moving into a new phase of my life felt right for family and me.

After meeting my son's dad when I was only 17 years old, the adjustment to becoming a newly single mum to a premature baby felt surreal. I had felt lost for several months until one evening I was contemplating the various things I could do for myself, mostly to get myself out of the hole I felt I was in. Work had taken its toll and drinking alcohol had become a regular occurrence to me in an attempt to numb my emotions. As I was sitting there, it came to me, visit a psychic a little voice in the back of my mind said. I came across the details of a local psychic medium online; I felt drawn to him out of the list of psychics I came across while scrolling. I had never had a reading before, and I didn't know what to expect; I was excited and nervous when I booked my session. The reading that I received blew my mind, and I talk about it regularly on my business platforms today. The psychic reading I received changed my life that day; it gave purpose and meaning to what had seemed like years of unhappiness. I started development sessions and quickly learned everything I could about tarot, psychic connections, connecting with spirit, and much more.

Throughout the initial developmental stage of my journey, I could feel that increasing my connection to spirit, and my own intuition was bringing me much closer to a place that felt like home. I loved every moment that I spent learning about the new and wonderful worlds of energy as well as the new practices that I could incorporate into my daily life. As my connection to myself and spirit deepened, I found that the beliefs and routines I once had such as; the thoughts on educational structures, the judgements I made about others, societal structures, beliefs around our government as well as my ability to watch TV and engage in meaningless chat changed. I no longer had an interest in joining the system that society had built around me. What I was starting to see was a deeply flawed system, one that had been created to demoralise, demotivate, and control society. I was moving further and further away from this, and my old belief system was starting to crumble. I found that I had become a slave to the confines of my own mind; somehow, society had placed me within an invisible prison; and I was finally breaking the chains; I was stepping out into a new world of infinite possibilities.

Once I had decided to take a step back from what society perceive as "the norm" such as; watching TV, engaging and following news headlines, and following mainstream trends, I could feel myself starting to stand in my own truth. I was starting to develop my own power, my own belief system; it was the most liberating and freeing feeling I had experienced. I was able to stand apart from others and feel confident in the belief system I now stood for. I was finally finding me, the real me.

Shortly after my belief systems started to shift, I began my inner healing journey. I had seen various different modalities that I could have started with such as shadow work, trauma therapy, quantum healing and reiki. I was drawn to trying a technique called emotion code which Dr Bradley Nelson has created; , it is a method of working within the quantum field to release trapped emotions. I soon got to work on finding a qualified practitioner. The sessions that I received through this only strengthened my connection to my inner being, and shortly after a block of sessions, I felt the urge to have regular Reiki sessions. Looking back now, I realise that the signs had been all around me for some time to start my healing journey, signs that had been unnoticeable to me.

After my course of Reiki sessions, I then dove headfirst deeply into the next phase of my healing journey. I started making my way through a process I had put in place for myself. Finally, I was connecting to parts of me that had been hidden for years, and I couldn't believe I unconditionally loved the hurt and the painful parts of myself that had been buried so deeply within me. This process highlighted the pain that I had tried so vigorously to ignore. I was beginning to understand the real meaning of life as I transitioned through the various stages within my own healing; most noticeably, I came to the understanding that earth is a large school for all of our souls; it is a training ground for us to heal our wounded and some-times broken hearts as well as self-growth for our soul and energetic bodies. I understood that the sculpture of my own being was down to me; I could do and achieve anything that I wanted, ultimately my potential in this lifetime was limitless and I was not going to let anything hold me back. I was no longer buying into the fear that had been woven so carefully into life as I had once known it.

Sometime after my healing journey began, I decided that I needed to stop drinking alcohol; the time felt right. I had never been ready;

alcohol was my final crutch. It seemed as though, relationship after relationship, I was being met with partners that suffered addictions. I had the misconception that I needed to help these partners see just how damaging their habits really were. Trying to help and change the other person became second nature to me. I wanted to help them see how badly their addiction had taken hold, all the while ignoring that it was, in fact, my own habits being mirrored back to me. It hit me; I needed to stop drinking for good.

Alcohol to me was an escape; I would use it as a way of switching off. If I was happy, I would drink, if I was sad, I would drink, if I was upset, I would drink. I decided that in order to fully face my fears as well as who I was at my absolute core, I had to stop drinking. I needed to stop hiding; I needed to stand out as me, fully open and vulnerable to the change that had now so quickly rippled through every corner of my life.

The shift that I experienced through stopping alcohol was immense; it had opened me up emotionally, and with this newfound freedom also came some deep inner child work that needed to be done. I was finally able to look and process the various traumas that I had faced and so naively ignored. I thought that trauma just was; I never knew that healing was ever an option. I had never been given the tools or strategies to cope with my pain which is why I drank so frequently. Around a month after cutting out all alcohol, I was able to feel everything that I had been suppressing. To my surprise, what came back was not only the painful memories but also the ability to feel deep and lasting joy, happiness and love; this process was transformational.

There was a period in my journey that I went through called the dark night of the soul; I was physically unable to work, this is a stage of deep transformation as everything you once knew sheds away and the new you is being created. A dark cloud hung over my head, and it wasn't shifting; I knew I needed to do work on myself in order to get through this stage, and I continued to do this in a number of different ways. This time in my life was a very painful experience as what came bubbling up to the surface were old memories, emotions, traumas and fears. I couldn't navigate this journey alone, so I enlisted coaches, teachers and mentors, as well as a number of different healing techniques to support my magnificent transition.

I had gained the awareness that I needed to hold onto my new belief structure and allow my inner compass to guide me further into my own greatness. A task that I grabbed firmly with two hands.

As my journey continued from strength to strength Archie felt that it was the right time to tell me that he himself had a memory that he wanted to share. Archie began to describe the moment of his birth, he explained in detail that he could see lots of crystals and emeralds all around us, flashes of light which he described as powers began floating into me; they were going into my throat, some into my legs and some into my arms, all coming down from the sky. Faces then appeared and said to him, "you have given birth to powers within your mother" he said that he could recall this as if it were yesterday, some of the faces were red, some were blue, and it was at this point he felt a vibration and that is when something hit him, he knew that he needed to use the powers that he had been given for the good of others. He described this as being his unforgettable memory. I was lucky enough at the time to start recording his experience so that we will always have this detailed and fascinating recollection of his birth; this confirmation is enough for me to know that everything I was experiencing all happened for a specific reason, to support and guide others.

My soul had started to speak to me; I was so far from the person that had started this journey some 6 years before; without a shadow of a doubt, what was happening to me was transformational, and an increasing sense of dis-ease was growing inside of me. Something didn't feel right; I knew that my job had fallen out of alignment with my soul over the previous months. It was leaving me feeling disappointment, stagnation and the growing urge to make a tremendous life shift in quitting my job was taking hold. Throughout all of these huge internal shifts that were taking place I had been growing my business as a Psychic Medium and Spiritual Teacher guiding others on their journey into self-discovery and as I strengthened my connection to spirit and my higher self, I knew ultimately that I had no other choice but to leave everything I'd known of my career for the last 12 years.

Immediately after handing my notice into work, and choosing to leave the rat race, I felt a sense of peace wash over my whole being. I was following my internal guidance towards what my soul had been preparing me to do. This was wholeheartedly the best decision I had ever made and the biggest intuitive urge that I had ever taken action upon. In the week that followed my resignation I could feel the final dark cloud lift and I was able to truly get started on my new journey and chapter within my life. A chapter that would go on to help others in the thousands.

The clients started to flow towards me with such ease; I could feel that supporting clients in their own journey and transformations was a very important aspect of my work. My work is inherently soul and spirit-led, meaning no two client programs are ever the same; this uniqueness is what my clients have given such positive feedback on. I work with clients on a long-term basis as well as shorter 6-weeks intensive development programs; through interaction with me, coupled with my teachings, my clients find significant growth and lasting growth. I work on an energetic level with the help of my spirit guides in the higher dimensions, raising the vibrations of my clients throughout our sessions; many of my clients note the new abilities that are activated within their souls very quickly after starting their first session.

I was called to put all of my teachings in one easily digestible book which is currently in the making. In July 2022 we will see the release of this book, Step Into the Light, the ultimate guide to understanding your spiritual awakening. The purpose of this book is to make my teachings easily accessible to everyone and to support those who have experienced a spiritual awakening. This book includes important techniques and stages that one transitions through along the spiritual path.

Throughout my learning journey, I have come to the understanding that Spiritual Teachers, Guides and Mentors are highly evolved souls that are here to support the growth of global conscious-ness and humanity; this can be done on a small or larger scale. There are various roles one can play in order to raise the vibrations of humanity, such as Healers, Mediums, Teachers, Artists, Environmen-talists, and Singers, to name a few. Any position that creates improve-ment of the world, service to others (as well as yourself) and brings forth positive change for future generations is where you will find your greatest passion.

There is no mistake that you are here reading this book today. Have you contemplated which stage you are currently at in your jour-ney? Is there a growing sense of dis-ease within you, wondering if there is more to life than this? Maybe you have just experienced a spiritual awakening and would like to know what comes next? The stages that lead to living a soul led life can be easily navigated with the right support and guidance from an experienced Teacher.

For me, beginning to live my life in a soul-led way has been life-changing; the transition highlighted how blindly miserable I had been while I was trapped in the constraints of societal programming. I am free, my soul is free and I am here on this Earth to help others remember at their core being what they came here to do. As I mentioned earlier, Earth is known as the training ground for our soul's growth, and we are here for this very reason, to find our true mission and gain the most growth possible in order to evolve.

My goal is to serve as a teacher and mentor for personal develop-ment and self-growth, catalysing individuals into their true poten-tial. I sit here now as I write this and thank the universe for allowing me to open up my gifts and psychic abilities in a way that can truly benefit and enrich the lives of many who reach out to me.

Whether you know your specific role at this time or not, have the awareness that we are all here to shape humanity, and each and every one of us has a very unique and magical part to play.

Are you ready to find yours?

ABOUT THE AUTHOR

SARAH NEWTON-SMITH

Sarah Newton-Smith is the founder of Sarah Smith Psychic. Sarah is passionate about her work as a Psychic Medium and Spiritual Teacher. Her purpose and mission is to guide others on their journey to enlightenment through transformation and self-development. Throughout her teachings, Sarah supports her clients in owning their modalities such as Remote viewing, Spirit connection, Psychic connection, Mediumship connection, Energy work, Soul repair, and Distance Healing. By sharing her knowledge with the world, Sarah can ensure that global transformations can continue. Having been through several life transformations Sarah draws on her experiences to empower her clients to use their personal power. Sarah is a mother of two and an avid nature enthusiast who lives in London with her German Shepherd, Rocco, and her two Bengal fur babies.

Website:
www.sarahsmithpsychic.com
Facebook:
www.facebook.com/StepIntoTheLightMedium

Instagram:
www.instagram.com/sarahsmithpsychic/

STACI LANE ALEXANDER

THE LANGUAGE OF LOVE

*H*ello!

My hope for writing this is that it finds you in a state of well-being.

I also have hope, more so have intention, that this book, this chapter, and these words, find you curious. Chances are, reading this book, you have found you are looking for something deeper. Maybe you are looking for answers to your problems, your feelings, the feelings of others, or your responsibility in it all. Or maybe these days, you are looking broader and deeper to unlock bigger questions, questions about life experience, about life purpose, or about the Universe.

If either of these or any of these are familiar, you are my people.

So hello, new friend. I'm so happy to have you here with me.

This chapter, the one you are just beginning to read right now, is purposefully written so that it feels just like a conversation between you and me as homies from way back.

Now that it's just you and me, I'd like to tell you a little, or a lot, about myself. Let's tap into the safe space I've created around my story. (Get cozy!)

Not too long ago, the best word to describe me in my situation was Lost. Lost in life, lost in relationships, lost in purpose

Dude. *So Lost.*

Another failed relationship was staring me in the face. I was in a constant state of irritation, and I felt I was unpleasant to be around because of it. I complained a lot about it. I complained a lot about a lot. I was unhealthy in every way. My mental body was in overdrive and burning out, my physical body starved of nutrients and affection, and my emotional body felt constantly backed in a corner. I was ready to pull out whichever trauma response was needed to survive, though, at the time, I didn't understand that this was what I was doing. Was it fight time? Flight? Would I completely tense up? Or would I give my power away to someone so they feel loved? As a single mom, I felt shame in my seeming lack of ability to parent well. I mean, I felt like I was doing alright? But in every move I made, people I held in close proximity would tell me I had no clue what I was doing, even after twenty years of working with children. I believed them.

Lost & Powerless.

I mean, I wasn't a total failure, per se. I was doing ok! I had lots of odd jobs to support my son and me. Most of the time, I was overly nice to appease others. I was over-giving, and I "loved really hard." I never argued with anyone after my marriage because it brought up so much pain. I would spend my free time socializing and over-drinking, getting myself in and out of "situation-ships" that never resulted in the love I was seeking. Choosing the wrong (but, oh, completely right) partners, deciding they were the ones that would get to hold my fragile heart. I would go against my gut in so many situations, trusting everyone other than myself to guide me in the right direction. I prided myself in my "free-flowing and easy-going" approach to life. I felt that this made a cool lady and a prize partner. Then why was I struggling so much? I was in a constant state of reaction to life.

I must have been speaking some prayers into existence because responses started to show up.

It was as if I became very aware, very rapidly, that I lived in a terrible headspace. A rude headspace. A negative headspace. I was awful to myself and tried so, so hard to be "The Love" for everyone else in my life.

This feeling was extremely disempowering, and it caused me to break down.

Side-note: Does this sound familiar to you? One of the hard parts about living this way is a lot of folks don't know they possess the power to change their lives. They don't even know there is any other way to live besides the way they've been living! I am here to tell you you can, and you will start changing your life once you come to the realization that it has to be YOU that makes the choice. No one else can, and no one else will save you.

I needed help. For the first time in my life, I allowed myself to say that out loud; actually, more like screamed it. For a whole week, I cried. I finally admitted that I hated my life, and I hated who I showed up as in life. I hadn't met my own feelings yet, hadn't allowed them to surface. Dude, I didn't even know what my feelings were; that's how much I ignored my own needs, wants, and desires. I ignored my Self.

I made tearful phone calls that I had put off for years, barely able to verbalize the words I was trying to say. "Please.... help me." Speaking these with such deep intention was magical, like suddenly being aware of previously invisible doors. These words were me finally realizing that this life isn't meant to be experienced isolated and alone. I was finally reaching out for connection- connection to myself and connection to others- and soon realized there are a vast amount of people waiting for me on the other side of my magic words. Shoot, I was waiting for me on the other side of them!

I was determined to do whatever it took to change my life. I started to attend therapy and spirit energy sessions bi-weekly. I began surrounding myself with people who were healing themselves and their lives, who weren't afraid to ask big questions. I began reading any and every book, article, and post that made me think about how I lived my life. I started to attend yoga classes, not because I actually desired to, but because I felt guided to go, and I listened to my inner guidance. I started to become very aware of how much and how little I was showing up as a parent, a friend, and an employee. I paid atten-tion to how my body reacted to people's presence. I continued to hone the importance of the superpower that we are all born doing-crying.

I started to have humongous emotional breakdowns and break-throughs.

Memories that had been tucked away in my subconscious started floating to the surface like ping pong balls refusing to be held down underwater. As each new/old memory popped up, instead of attempting desperately to push it back down, so I didn't have to confront it, I'd pull it to the forefront of my thoughts and hold it for the first time ever. This meant for some really low days, allowing deep grief, fear, anger, shame, and guilt to wash over and through me. But I started to observe that the pain always led to something wonderful, like a rainbow after a storm. After I experienced the (sometimes massive) discomfort in uncovering some of my old ways of thinking and being and would allow myself to process, I would come out of the other side a little more peaceful.

I would come out of the situation with just a little more Love.

This was a new feeling for me, this love. I felt that I had always been a loving person, but before only allowed myself to find and see it through other people. When I would put myself around others who couldn't do a good job of showing or reciprocating love, I felt that it must be because I wasn't worthy, or well behaved enough, to deserve it. Suddenly that old way of loving myself seemed most unhealthy and unhelpful. This new way of processing was so much more beneficial to me. I started to build my self-love brick by brick.

What I didn't understand then and see so clearly now was that my foundation of safe, solid love wasn't built strong. I'm not sure I was given the right tools as a child, and as a result, all the other pieces got built on top of this rocky foundation. I just kept recreating scenarios over and over again to try to find the love I so desperately needed and wanted. It's like building an entire house on top of an unstable foundation. It won't last long, and if the wind blows too hard, it's all coming crumbling down, along with everything and everyone inside!

So off I went, building piece by piece, emotion by emotion,

thought by thought. As I started to deepen into my practice of observing myself, the Universe started to mirror my intention and offer me situation after situation of more opportunities to flex my newfound skills. And FLEX I friggin' have, friend.

One new set of skills was me learning and placing boundaries where none existed. A big lesson I learned: Not everyone is down with the new boundaries! Most especially the people that were taking advantage of the lack of boundaries I had before! I learned that not everyone signs up for my betterment and that not everyone likes it when I grow, and it reflects they haven't. Boundaries are a challenge at first but become easier to establish the more they are practiced.

Another skill was being so observant of my reactivity to life. When someone would say something that felt hurtful, my newfound skill was to do what yoga teaches and "find the pause." Instead of immediately reacting to situations with defensiveness, or the need to make sure no one had any reason to be upset with me (I had some spectacular people-pleasing tendencies ingrained in my psyche), I would take a few moments to let the words I have just received marinate. Percolate. Levitate. From here, I could respond, instead of reacting, in a more thoughtful way. I use this skill in all areas and relationships in life, especially the most triggering ones with loved ones.

What I really was doing was working through the life-altering concept of non-attachment. I started to see that people's words and actions were simply a reflection of themselves and their own emotional backgrounds and baggage. I didn't have to or need to attach my own stories to their actions, but simply observed them as doing the same thing as me- *Humaning*. OH, MAN! We are all out here just *HUMANING*! If I was experiencing and processing life, it makes sense to me that others were doing the same thing. We are all on different levels but playing the same game- the game of *Humaning* in Life. With this information and understanding of non-attachment, life seemed to have found a little more ease.

I have realized that my inner guidance system will never lead me astray. There are powers (I love referring to this as real-life magic) within me and reflected to me, that whisper in my ear. I have learned to listen to the tiny nudges as much as listening to the loud ones. I have learned that my inner guidance is an internal compass, and it's specifically designed just for me and my life experience. This doesn't mean I avoid tough situations, but it does mean that I will know that I can handle what feels like I can't.

After some outside encouragement, I decided to start to learn energy work so that I could understand myself more and then turn around and help others. It honestly scared me because I didn't understand much about it and had to learn by throwing myself into fires only to see that I was the Phoenix, and nothing could or would take me down. This, I understand, is courage: facing fear and walking toward it. I started to feel the energy in my body with intentionality and worked to harness it. I started to deepen into listening to my inner guidance, paying close attention to small details, gifts, and signs offered by the Universe. (Though I do not believe they are one and the same, the term "God" can be spoken interchangeably for Universe here. I do not usually use "God" when writing because religion's meaning and my meaning may not coincide.)

I have learned I can let new energy into my life, but first, "old" energy must be cleaned up. Maybe an easier way to grasp this concept is thinking about clearing it out, but really, it's transmutation and integration. This is still one of my favorite practices in my life. I delete people off social media that feel heavy and don't resonate with my broader belief system. I get rid of items in my house that, when I look at them, bring me back to a time and a place that I don't want to think about; I feel extra relief to get rid of items that are correlated with people from the past. I observe old survival patterns and old ways of thinking and change them. I purify my living, working, playing, and sleeping spaces with sage and intention. I slow down. I breathe intentionally. I play. I sing. I wiggle. I snuggle. I love.

And the biggest gift I give myself (and then ultimately to others) is the space to feel my feelings.

Having awareness, acceptance, and authority over our emotions: the movement of energy.

Negative feelings are keys. Let's refer to them as contrasting emotions because they are neither good nor bad, just energy ideally moving through. They are the information you can tap into. From my interpretation, they tend to live in the body, whether it's processed or not. They will not always be easy or feel good to become aware of. Sometimes it will feel downright scary for the awareness of the feeling to show up, let alone stepping into and confronting your own feelings. It's good to remember that there is always, as I see it, ALWAYS new knowledge, or growth, after the processing of emotion. And what's one way that we've already talked about to process emotion? YEP, you guessed it! The superpower of crying. That salt-water was gifted to us with purpose.

Once you understand that feelings are information to you, you can harness the power of understanding them and their purpose so much more. You will no longer feel like something is wrong with you when you aren't feeling your brightest. Please, friend, do not compare yourself to others. You are not them, and they are not you. You live a different life as a different human, so attempting to compare you with anyone else is like comparing my adorable cat to the wooden desk at which I sit. You have your own journey to make here, and it is unmatched by anyone else's. There is only one you. You must go within to truly find yourself. You must peel back layers to find the love that not only do you have, but that you ARE.

I will tell you this. You are meant for so much more. You are meant for absolute greatness in this life experience because you are absolute greatness. And if you don't see it right at this moment, don't you worry, because someone like me can already see it. Someone right now can already see you for who you really are and can hold that energetic frequency for you to get yourself into. It's the frequency of Love, my Love.

Love is what we are. Connected is what we came to be.

You are loved, you are loving, and you are LOVE.

You are a perfectly imperfect human, sometimes smooth sailing around life, sometimes fumbling to find the light switch to turn the strobe off. These are both ok. It's ok to stumble. It's ok not to be ok for a little bit. Take a break. Take a breather. Come back ready.

This I believe with my entire being because I have taken myself through this very journey. I have seen the butterfly emerge from the cocoon. And because I have seen such a difference in myself and the way I view others and the way I view life, I just know, in the core of my being, that this message applies to you too.

I guess I should update you on what life looks like now, right? So you can see the current "end result?" Well, I am continuing to be human, just like everybody else. My self-love has grown so deep as I have grown into my authentic self. I resonate so deeply in this self-love and self-trust energy and show up so much more whole-y for my child and many other children. I can lead through example and love. I can appreciate that others, too, are *humaning*. I hold a safe space for this to happen. I have found my calling, possibly my greater purpose in life. I have found peace through heartbreak. I've felt vast amounts of grief and joy. I ebb and flow with part grace, part wild fury, because that's just a part of who I am. I surround myself with incredible women and men who can hold space for me, which is the truest act of kindness.

I feel, I shift, I grow. I help others feel, shift, and grow when they are ready. I still spend hours and hours with children in a capacity that truly meets my heart's needs, and I trust it does theirs as well. I live life as I want to, as what serves me here forward.

And I guide others to do the same.

This is my story, but it could be your story too.

That's why I wrote this.

I want you to know that

You don't always have to live life on the edge. You don't have to isolate, and you don't have to accept your story as is.

You are not alone. You can't be alone when you have a connection to your Self. Love your Self.

Are you ready?

Are you ready to meet who you really are? Are you ready to see what you are truly capable of achieving in your life? Within your relationships? *There is Hope.*

I can't wait to hear your story.

Until then,

All my Love and thanks for being here with me.

SA

ABOUT THE AUTHOR

STACI LANE ALEXANDER

Staci Alexander is the Owner & Artistic Director of The Creative Movement, a collective wellness-through-movement company! The mission statement is "Providing a safe space for everyone to explore movement within their bodies." Staci combines her career of professional dance and theater with her love for all things energetics and emotional intelligence. Reiki, Intuitive guidance, and the Emotion Code are three ways she works with women ready to step closer to their authentic selves so they can tap into their highest potential & show up as who they are for the betterment of their lives. Staci was named "Life Coach of the Year" in 2021 by her community just because of her uplifting and authentic view of life and human experiences and recording them online. She resides in Maryland by the beach, along with her son and their two fur turkeys (cats), Penelope & Telle.

Facebook:
https://www.facebook.com/TheCreativeMovementisNow
Instagram:
http://www.instagram.com/staci_with_an_eye1111
Email:
Thecreativemovement2014@gmail.com

ABOUT THE PUBLISHER

SANCTUARY PUBLISHING & ANNETTE MARIA

*S*anctuary Publishing was birthed out of a desire for our stories to be treated as sacred. Back in 2017, Annette received a channeled idea in the middle of an anxiety attack about a children's book called the Worry Wave. The Worry Wave is a beautiful story teaching children how to navigate their emotions and move through comparison. In her quest for getting published, she felt that her sacred story was just treated like another business transaction but didn't know where else to turn. Once the Worry Wave became published, Annette felt an urge to do things differently.

For those big dreams of being published to be truly celebrated and for the words written to be honored in a sacred birthing process. Sanctuary Publishing is here to do publishing with purpose. We highlight authors who are out in the world making a difference through their soul medicine to further reach the masses. They are the change makers, visionaries, and thought leaders that are rooted in bringing more love and peace to the planet.

Through multi-author books, solo-author books, and oracle/tarot card creation, we work with the mystical, spiritually driven leaders to bring their medicine even further out into the world.

If you resonate with Sanctuary Publishing and have a creation you wish to birth into the world, please email Annette Maria, hello@ activationsbyannette.com. She will get back to you to feel into further alignment of working together.

Other ways to connect with Annette Maria:

Website:

Activationsbyannette.com/publishing

Instagram:

https://www.instagram.com/its.annettemaria/

Facebook:

https://www.facebook.com/annettemaria123

LinkedIn:

https://www.linkedin.com/in/annetteszproch/

Insight Timer:

https://insig.ht/OKaCbZzTFkb?utm_source=copy_link& utm_medium=live_stream_share

The Worry Wave Children's Book:

The Worry Wave

Printed in Poland
by Amazon Fulfillment
Poland Sp. z o.o., Wrocław

94248975R00096